More Tales of Old Chesham

By
George Piggin

George Best wishes

George Piggin

Highgate of Beverley

Highgate Publications (Beverley) Limited
1995

British Library Cataloguing in Publication Data.
A catalogue record for this book is available from the British Library.

© 1995 George Piggin

ISBN 0 948929 90 1

Published by

Highgate of Beverley
Highgate Publications (Beverley) Limited
24 Wylies Road, Beverley, HU17 7AP
Telephone (01482) 866826

Produced by

4 Newbegin, Lairgate, Beverley, HU17 8EG
Telephone (01482) 886017

Front Cover Picture: Red Lion Street, 1935.

CONTENTS

PREFACE

My last book – *Tales of Old Chesham* – was published in 1993, and was very well received. I have had many appreciative comments, and know that copies have been despatched to former Chesham residents now living in many parts of the world, and many of these have been passed on to people who had never heard of the place – so perhaps I am unwittingly promoting the town!

I am still speaking to groups and societies on the subject, and have bookings for the next year. Many times have I been asked, 'Are you writing another book – there must be many more stories worth telling?' Six months ago I got down to it, and the following chapters are the result. I have tried to tell, as last time, of things long forgotten by most; some tales I hope will re-kindle memories; some are too far in the past.

Once again, I am indebted to photographer Ray East for many of the pictures; it is truly amazing what is still around when one starts enquiring! I am also grateful, for their comments and advice on past events and societies, to Ray Edmunds, Terry Howard, Sheila Taylor, Harry Wing, Horace Smith, Ernie Russell and Cecil Monk. Their help was freely given. Sincere thanks also to Jennifer Marsh for typing and putting into good order all my ramblings.

My hope now is that my readers will gather a few more facts concerning Chesham's fascinating past.

George Piggin
Amy Lane
Chesham
April 1995

1. The Town Gas Works

Today, as we use our gas cookers, fires and central heating, few of us give a thought as to where the gas actually comes from; by the time it reaches our homes it has come literally hundreds of miles, from under the North Sea via the pipelines of the National Grid. What a difference to half a century ago – and indeed for a hundred years previous to that – when all of Chesham's gas was produced locally.

In 1846 a group of local men got together and formed the Chesham Gas Company. Gas was then a comparatively recent introduction – let us remember that prior to that time the only lighting in houses was by paraffin lamps or candles. Lamps were dirty, smoky things, which had to be cleaned and filled every day. Street lighting was almost non-existent – just an odd oil lamp, which gave very little illumination, at some street corners. The Gas Company raised funds by issuing shares to the public, and for many years these shares were much prized by the holders as they always paid a regular dividend of 3 or 4 per cent, which at the time was always considered a good investment which was completely safe, as indeed it was.

The gas works were erected in Waterside, at the corner of Hospital Hill, with the gasometers (or gas holders) at the rear. Sad to say, all that remains today is the Manager's house, a rather delightful small listed building. The retorts (where the gas was made) were in due course erected in a high roofed building, and a web of pipes was gradually spread under the roads and pavements all over the town, to supply the various shops, factories, houses and street lights. The gas was, of course, for years produced from coal, which originally had to be brought by horse-drawn cart from the nearest railway station – until 1889, Berkhamsted. This was a very slow and costly operation. When Chesham Station opened in 1889 this eased things considerably, and the horse and cart laden with coal became a familiar sight as it trundled its way from the goods yard, down White Hill and through High Street to Waterside. In the 1920s, the horse and cart were superseded by a large open lorry – a solid tyred job for years, which bumped its way down the street, often shedding lumps of coal which were gathered up by boys with trucks.

Coke and Tar, both by-products of the gas manufacture, were always available for sale at the Gas Works, the former for banking up your fire, as it was

GAS WORKS HOUSE

1

RETORTS AT THE GAS WORKS

slow burning, and the latter for painting on to sheds, fences, and indeed on to a few wooden houses in the town – a good coat of tar was thoroughly waterproof and long lasting, if a bit messy to apply! It had to be boiled over a fire to make it thin enough to handle, and application with a brush was rather hard work.

In the 1920s the Gas Company lost the street lighting contract to the Electricity Company, and, following nationalisation in the early 1950s, the local Gas Works closed down. Today, we have recently even lost our Gas Showrooms in the High Street, our nearest being at Hemel Hempstead. Do things get any easier?

2. The Electricity Works

Following the discovery of electricity in the late 1800s most towns and cities began to develop and provide their own systems of supply. Prior to this discovery, of course, the only means of lighting in homes, shops and factories was by gas or oil lamps, and such street lighting as there existed was gas. A Chesham Electricity Company was set up in 1904 – one of the earliest in the district, and a generating works at Higham Mead (off Higham Road) was erected.

The brains behind the project was the man who became Chief Engineer, Mr. R. J. J. Swan, who oversaw the erection of the plant and the subsequent supply system to most parts of the town. This was a slow process, as the streets had to be dug up for the cables to be laid, and overhead wires on poles erected as the supply spread to outlying parts. Mr. Swan was ably assisted by his Engineer, Mr. 'Dick' Clayton, a heavily built man who stood some 6ft 5 inches tall, and it was always a source of amazement to onlookers to see Dick lower himself down to deal with a matter requiring attention in an underground chamber! Gradually, the new idea caught on and more and more homes received the benefit of electric lighting. Cookers were not, of course, heard of at this time! However, at the time of writing – ninety years later – there are still a few homes in the town lit by gas, and it is good to know that our wonderful local ironmonger – Pearce's – still stocks gas mantles!

In the 1920s there was a prolonged battle between the Gas Company (who already had the contract) and the Electricity Company for the street lighting of the town. The latter company eventually won, and

CHESHAM ELECTRICITY POWER STATION – EARLY 1900s.

gradually the new system took over. For a good number of years the lamps had to be turned on and off by the company's lamplighter – a similar man, of course, existed in gaslit days. The big lamps in the High Street were turned on individually at dusk and off at 11 p.m., but the smaller lamps in the side streets were grouped together with switch boxes at appropriate points. There were a considerable number of these situated around the town. At various junctions – Broadway, Market Square etc. – a single light was left on until 1 a.m., to cater for those people coming off the last train from London, which arrived at the station a few minutes earlier. There was invariably a mad rush to get home before the last bit of illumination disappeared!

Chesham's system was in due course extended to cover both Berkhamsted and Chesham Bois, neither of which had its own system. The local Company remained independent until 1925, when it was taken over by METESCO – the Metropolitan Electricity

Supply Company – although a large measure of independence still remained. Later, on nationalisation of the industry, this was taken over by the Eastern Electricity Board.

One feature of the Works will long be remembered – the siren, or Shrieking Lizzie as it was always known; this was fixed to the chimney at the end of the building, and was used as the town fire alarm; it had a truly penetrating sound, and could be heard all over the town. It was tested at 12 noon every Saturday, and was sounded to call the firemen to the Fire Station in the event of a fire. It was not, however, sounded between the hours of 10 p.m. and 7 a.m. – that would have been too much! During those hours the firemen were deemed to be at home, and an alarm sounded in their houses.

I know that these days we get good service from Eastern Electricity, but cannot nevertheless help but feel it a pity that all these services have passed out of local hands!

3. The River Chess

Most of us are familiar with our local river, the Chess, as it flows through the town, although it is principally visible only in the lower parts – Moor Road, Waterside, and Latimer Road. However, I wonder how many of us are familiar with its course from its sources?

Contrary to many expressed opinions, the river takes its name from the town, and not the other way round!

The farthermost source is at Higham Mead (behind Higham Road), now largely built over with factories, but only a century ago an area of watercress beds – just some of Chesham's many – and also the site of Chesham's first cricket ground. The tributary is visible as it passes under Higham Road and under Townsend Road, after which it completely disappears into a culvert for a considerable distance. It passes under Great Mills, Albany Place car park, the Malt House and offices nearby, then crosses under the lower end of Blucher Street and under Broadway Baptist Church. It then passes underground at the rear of the properties on the west side of the High Street, and can be seen through a grating at the rear of the George Hotel. It then crosses under Church Street, under the properties on the west side of the Market Square, and crosses under Germain Street from Wright's to the Red Lion. It then crosses under the site of the old printing works, and joins the main stream at the foot of the once-named Duck Alley (so named, of course, because ducks were once kept there and swam on the river). We hope that Duck Alley may soon be re-instated as a riverside walk! It is almost certain that, before the days of public water supply and main drainage, the properties in the High Street – then almost all were private houses – drew their water from the stream and also used it for the disposal of household waste and other unmentionables!

THE CHESS AT CHESHAM MOOR IN ITS HALCYON DAYS

A second tributary springs forth on opposite sides of the lower Pednor Road, about half a mile out of the town; one side becomes Bury Lake, and the other side, after forming two one-time watercress beds, crosses under the roadway and also joins Bury Lake. At the lower end of this lake one exit again crosses Pednor Road, under the buildings at the lower end of Church Street, and emerges by the side of the Queen's Head. The other exit also crosses Pednor Road, passes the tennis courts, then curls round, crossing Missenden Road and Church Street to join the stream mentioned above under the roadway, thence emerging by the side of the Queen's Head. The third tributary arises opposite Half Way House Farm in Missenden Road, and proceeds through the meadows to join the stream coming from Pednor Road near the tennis courts. From the Queen's Head the stream is visible throughout, traversing Water Lane, Germain Street, thence by the Meades Water Gardens, under Amersham Road by Banaglaze Works and thence alongside Moor Road. Beyond the present railway bridge, the river was diverted in the 1600s to provide a head of water for Lords Mill – the original route followed the twisting nature of the present road as far as the swimming pool, where nowadays the overflow from the Weir by Kitty's Bridge passes under the road; this in turn joins the main stream by Nor-Jo-An Villas.

For hundreds of years the Chess provided the motive power for our mills – the mill in Water Lane, Amen, Lords, Cannon, Weir House and Bois Mills; only the two last-named are now visible, although neither, of course, now used for its original purpose. I have several times been questioned by older residents who say that they remember, years ago, seeing barges tied up alongside Moor Road; I am afraid that this is a fallacy – such vessels could never have passed under the low buildings of the mills.

Boating of a sort – for pleasure – certainly took place on the wide stretch of water between the railway and Kitty's Bridges, before that lovely stretch was allowed by the local authority to silt up so badly; at one time the bed of this stretch was regularly cleared of mud, but eventually the clearance ceased, and the reed beds gradually grew into the island and its present overlarge size – but at least it provides a haven and nesting place for ducks, geese and swans which it never originally did!

4. Dentistry a Century Ago

I think that the following advertisement from the *Chesham Examiner* of June, 1891, is well worthy of reproduction:

Dental Surgery and Artificial Teeth
8 High Street, High Wycombe
Established nearly a Quarter of a Century
MR. EDWARD MAWER
(Late of the Dental Hospital and R.D.S. of the Royal College of Surgeons)
RESIDENT SURGEON DENTIST
Attends Chesham every Thursday from 12 to 4 o'clock at 10 High Street

The Artificial Teeth perfected by Mr. Mawer are the most life-like ever yet produced. They are artistic and natural in form, and give to the face a pleasing and charming character, and the appearance of artificiality is entirely avoided.

The prices charged by Mr. Mawer are in every case based upon most moderate computation, and he is in a position to give really the best work for about one-fourth the fees charged by many.

Here are the greatest facilities for obtaining EVERY POSSIBLE KIND AND CLASS OF TEETH from the MOST ARTISTIC AND PERFECT to the MOST MODERATE AND INEXPENSIVE.

CONSULTATIONS FREE – Explanatory pamphlet gratis on application to above address.

Nitrous Oxide Gas, Ether and also Cocaine administered for painless operations.

5. Disatrous Fire in the Broadway

I feel that the following is worthy of recalling – what a night in Chesham! From the *Chesham Examiner, Amersham and Rickmansworth Times* of 3 June, 1891: One of the most serious fires with which Chesham has been visited in recent years took place on Sunday night last, when one of the Business Establishments situated in that portion of the High Street known as the Broadway was entirely burnt out, and the adjoining property partially so. About 5 minutes past Ten o'clock dense volumes of smoke were observed issuing forth from the house and shop occupied by Mr John Thomas, Tailor and Outfitter, and situate at the corner of Station Road. Flames were first seen at the back of the premises, but almost immediately after they were noticed to come through the fanlight over the shop door, the heat cracking and breaking the glass. News of the outbreak was then speedily conveyed in all directions, and the fire bell at the Town Hall was rung for several minutes. The inhabitants in the majority of cases had not retired to rest, and on hearing the alarm great numbers of them rushed out of their houses to ascertain where the fire was. "Thomas's in The Broadway is ablaze!" was heard on all hands, and the reflection of the flames indicated only too plainly the truthfulness of this remark. People who had gone to bed got up, and made their way to the scene of the outbreak. The thoroughfare here being very wide, there was ample room for the great crowds of spectators who assembled. The Fire Brigade were called, and the whole of the members (with one exception) were quickly at the Fire, under the command of Captain Stone. The Brigade first obtained their hose truck, with five lengths of hose. The truck is usually kept in the Corn Exchange, but when that building is let for a Sale the truck has to be removed. This was the case on the present occasion, and there was a little delay in getting the truck out of the Yard (in the Market Square) in which it was placed, the gates being locked. The hose cart was taken to the Broadway, and three more lengths of hose, which were in the Engine House, were also sent for and brought into requisition. In the meantime a Messenger was dispatched to the Waterworks with direction to the person in charge to start the engines, so as to secure a full supply in the mains. We may here state that, had there not been a constant supply instead of an intermittent one (as had obtained for a few months), the fire would have been far more serious in its consequences than it proved to be. The firemen attempted to affix the hose to the nearest standpipe, but something was the matter with the hydrant and they could not get the hose affixed to it. They then tried the standpipe near to the residence of Mr. Churchill, and having got the hose affixed they were able to play on the flames. After doing this for a short time, the crowd, whilst in the act of shifting the hose, pulled the flange off the hydrant, rendering it useless. Steps were next taken to obtain water from the standpipe near to the residence of Mr. W. Webb, and from there a good supply was forthcoming, as long as it was required. The scene immediately after this almost baffles description. The premises of Mr. Thomas were almost totally alight from top to bottom, and the building was a mass of raging fire and resembled a huge furnace. Mr. Thomas' tenancy of the premises had nearly expired, – as a matter of fact he had removed a few of his things to another house he had taken in New Town. With the exception of a sewing machine, however, the whole of the contents of the house and shop in the Broadway were consumed. No sooner was the fire discovered than the whole place was enveloped in flames, so that no attempt could be made to save the contents. Next door to the consumed building is the Chesham Coffee Tavern, which was occupied by Mr. W. Ivory and his wife and family. The inmates here were quickly aroused and left the house, which it was feared would also fall prey to the devouring element. Adjoining the Coffee Tavern is a house occupied by Mr. Pearce and his family. One of these, Miss Pearce, was ill at the time and she was conveyed to the residence of Mr. G. Webb, where she was kindly received and taken every care of. Mr. W. O. Harding, Ironmonger, has the adjoining premises, and from here a quantity of Gunpowder and Oils was removed to a place of safety. Mr. W. Payne's new premises are next to those of Mr. Harding, and at one time it was feared that the fire would extend as far as here. Hence ensued a scene of wild confusion, bordering on a panic. The furniture and contents of the Coffee Tavern and Mr. Pearce's house were removed and stored in the open street and in the premises of some of the residents who dwell on the opposite side of the road. But in the removal of the goods great recklessness was exhibited by many who took part in the work. Furniture and crockery ware were thrown from the windows indiscriminately, much unnecessary damage being

thereby occasioned. Mr. Payne, fearing that the whole block of buildings would be consumed, allowed his shop to be nearly emptied of its contents, and the damage he has sustained amounts to over £10. Mr. Pearce estimates his loss at a sum much larger then this, while Mr. Ivory was not able to get all his rooms cleared, a portion of the furniture in the top rooms being burnt.

The firemen, as soon as they arrived at the scene, found that it would be useless to attempt to save the house in which the fire originated. The premises were burning fiercely, and it was patent to all that their destruction was only a question of time – and that only

MR. THOMAS' SHOP AFTER THE FIRE

a short one. The Brigade, therefore, set to work to cut off all communication, with a view to saving them. At one time the task seemed a hopeless one. Flames burnt through the roof of the Coffee Tavern, and on breaking down a partition with their hatchets they found themselves face to face with the fire in the roof. There was no party wall, so that the fire was able to run along the roof from the adjoining building. The hose was taken through the upstairs window of the Coffee Tavern, and handed to the firemen inside, who played on the flames. In the meantime some of the hose was taken round to the back of the premises, and by means of a second delivery water was poured on to the seat of the fire from this direction also. The firemen worked very hard for an hour and a half, and were assisted by numbers of the townspeople, included among the helpers being some of the most influential residents. About 11.30 it was found that the fire had been got under, and that there was no likelihood of it extending. By this time Mr. Thomas' house was completely gutted. Shortly before, the front wall fell down with a crash, and instantly people turned pale with fear. Was anyone injured by the falling debris? was the question on their lips, and when it was found that no-one had been hurt there was a great sense of relief.

Just before this wall fell, the fire was at its grandest. Flames – great, bright and roaring, issued from the burning mass with dense volumes of smoke. The wind carried these and the sparks straight across the roadway, and, had the thoroughfare not been unusually wide, one of the houses on the opposite side could scarcely have escaped. The reflection from the fire caused the firemen, spectators and surrounding property to stand out in bold relief; the public were enabled to watch the movements of the Brigade, while the flames caused a lurid glare to spread over the sky above, illuminating the scene, and making the presence of a fire known a long distance off. When the flames issued from the roof of the Coffee Tavern the outlook was one of grave apprehension, but owing to the exertions of the firemen the threatened danger was averted. A portion of the roof and two rooms and a

staircase at the Coffee Tavern were burnt out, and the roof of the building was damaged by fire, water and breakages. For some time after the fire had been got under control, the firemen continued to pour water on the burning debris, and the body of the men did not leave until between 2 and 3 o'clock. Some of the brigade remained on duty all night, and until nearly 10 o'clock on Monday morning firemen were present, some fire being found to exist under the mass of burning material as late as this. Captain Stone and his men worked well, and much credit is due to them for the exertions they made, which were crowned with so much success!! The Captain had a providential escape of a serious accident, his helmet being much bent by some falling brickwork. Fireman Hearne fell through a roof and hurt his knee, and other members of the Brigade had narrow escapes. The Police rendered what assistance they could, but we are afraid that they were unable to prevent pillage and robbery from taking place. A dog belonging to Mr. Thomas was injured by the fire. On Monday and Tuesday the scene of the fire was an object of much curiosity. Mr. Thomas' premises were a mass of ruins, blackened and charred. The front shop and two rooms on the ground floor with a sitting room and three bedrooms on the first floor (the house being one storey high) with the contents etc. were all totally consumed, the wall (which was new) separating the property from Station Road alone remaining. The property, which had a frontage to the Broadway of about 24 feet, was owned by Mr. James Reynolds, while the owner of the Coffee Tavern is Mr. J. W. Reading. Mr. Reynolds is insured with the County Fire Office, and Mr. Reading in the Royal Exchange. Mr. Thomas and Mr. Ivory are both insured in the Alliance Office. The total damage is estimated at about £1000.

6. Cricket in the 1890s

In the *Chesham Examiner* of 3 June, 1891, are reported – at length – two of Chesham's matches – one victory and one defeat.

Against Neasden at Home, the Visitors won the toss and put Chesham in to bat. Catling, who opened the Innings, made 9; then came a stand of 50 between Batchelor, who made 20, and Woodbridge, who it was stated had come a long way from Iver to play, who made 30. The other eight batsmen produced six runs between them, and the Innings closed for 68. Neasden were dismissed for 34, Extras being the highest score with 8. Chesham then went in for Second Innings and were dismissed for 30, Woodbridge again being top scorer – with six. Neasden then took their Second Innings, being dismissed for 34, leaving Chesham the victors by 30 runs.

The game against High Wycombe, Away, was a different story. The Home side batted first, and made – for those days – a very large score of 167. Chesham were dismissed for just 37 in the first Innings, W. Spearing being top scorer with 19, and for 117 in the second Innings, H. Webb making 40 and Catling 35, leaving High Wycombe the winners by an Innings and 13 runs.

Chesham St. Mary's C.C. were also featured in the same edition of the paper; they had played Holmer Green at Home. The visitors batted first and made 17 (top score 6) and St. Mary's replied with 43 (H. Smith 15). Holmer Green fared little better in their Second Innings – 36 all out, top score 9 – and St. Mary's knocked off the runs required for victory – 11 – for the loss of four wickets. The report says that the winning runs were scored 'With Great Excitement'.

Let us remember that cricket grounds – and particularly the wickets – were not quite of the standard which exists today!

7. Relief of the Poor in Pre-Social Security Days

Further snippets from the Parish Records:

John Grover Shop Keeper was buried in Linnen October 16th 1687 and his daughter informed Mr. Anderson the Justice thereof this day and year aforesaid and there was paid according to the Act Fiftie Shillings to Mr. Ivory and Overseer for the relief of the Poor as he thought fit to distribute.

Abraham Axtell Mercer was wrapped up in Linnen and buried the 13th day of June 1687 and informed Mr. Fleetwood the Justice by his son in law Daniell Roberts of the same this day and year aforesaid for which was paid according to the Act Fiftie Shillings to Samuell Page the Overseer for the relief of the Poor and distributed as he thought most fit and convenient.

Rebeccah Wife of Daniel Roberts Mercer was wrapped up in Linnen and buried the 18th day of February 1688 and I was informed of the same by Mr. John Chase Senior this day and year aforesaid for which was paid according to the Act Fiftie Shillings for the relief of ye poor and distributed by ye Overseers as they thought most fit and convenient.

(It appears that the relief of the Poor of the Parish depended to some extent on the number of Burials at the time!)

8. Harvesting

The gathering of the annual corn harvest today is a very simple, quick, and labour-saving exercise compared to that in the early 1900s – and indeed up until the immediate post-war years. This was brought about by the introduction of the combine harvester, a machine which was developed in America to ease the enormous operations which were necessary to gather the harvest from the vast American and Canadian prairies. Nowadays, provided that the weather is good and the corn dry, a fair sized field can be completely cleared in a day by only two or three men – one driving the combine; one driving the tractor and trailer to cart the harvested corn to the store; and one to operate the straw bailer. Harvest time, of course, seems to grow ever earlier with the development of quicker ripening varieties of corn – the season commences in July and is finished – weather permitting – by mid to late August.

Before this wonderful invention, the season rarely commenced before late August and dragged on until

*CORN STOOKS IN A
FIELD ON
DUNGROVE FARM*

THRESHING MACHINE

late September – and often into October – with ever shortening days making the task more and more difficult – and that was only the first part of the harvest operation. Until the invention almost a century earlier of the reaper and binder – a machine drawn by one horse, and which cut the corn, tied it into sheaves, and threw them out at the rear, all corn had to be cut by men with scythes, which needed constant sharpening due to the toughness and dryness of the corn stalks, and then tied into bundles by men following behind. The tied bundles were then gathered and built into wigwam-shaped stooks, with the corn heads uppermost, and they stood there until completely dry. A story regarding oats was that they had to stand there for at least three Sundays, as it was said that they needed to hear the church bells rung three times before being dry!

The sheaves were then picked up by horse and cart and conveyed to the Rick Yard, where a gang of men built them into a rick, which was raised off the ground on a platform of logs supported by staddle stones – this was to prevent vermin entering the rick. The sheaves were conveyed on to the ever-growing rick by means of a horse-operated elevator. Men on top with pitchforks would build the rick into shape, and, when it reached a height of some 12 to 15 feet, it was tapered off and thatched with straw (to keep out the rain) and left. Some time during the winter a threshing machine, drawn by a steam engine (which would provide the motive power) would arrive, with its gang of men – about a dozen were needed for the operation. One local machine was owned by Ned Gomm, of Pednor Road, who operated at many local farms during the threshing season.

The thatch was then removed from the rick, and two or three men perched on top would pitchfork the sheaves into the threshing machine, from which would emerge the corn – straight into sacks – through one aperture, and the straw from another into an ever growing heap. This was then gathered up and tied by hand into trusses, which was used for winter bedding at the farm and also sold to stables and poultry keepers.

In spite of precautions, the base of the rick was invariably frequented by rats and mice, and, as the pile grew ever smaller, they would emerge to be shot at by men with guns and ever active dogs.

9. Old Rubbish Dumps

Until the setting up of our local Council a century ago, the disposal of domestic waste was very much a do-it-yourself affair. Admittedly, compared with the present day, the amount of waste was tiny – packaging had just not been heard of! Your principal waste was the ashes from your fireplace each morning, and these were thrown on to your garden, where they provided valuable fertiliser in the form of potash. Any food wrapping was invariably old newspaper, which could be burned on your fire. As non-destructible packaging came into use – notably food cans and bottles – their disposal began to be a problem. A weekly collection by horse and uncovered cart was set up by the Urban District Council, and somewhere near to the town had to be found to dump the stuff. Our first dump – which lasted about 20 years – was in the dell off Asheridge Road; when this became filled, our next site was a dell off Upper Pednor Road – at the corner of Blind Lane. This lasted until the late 1920s; the site is now covered with a coppice of fir trees. The town had by this time grown considerably, and the amounts of rubbish were rapidly increasing. The Council hit upon the idea of using the Lower Moor. The entire length of this – from Moor Road right down to Cannon Mill – was an area of marshland, growing nothing but reeds and marsh grass. Carts began to trundle through the town – by 1930 to be replaced by motor lorries; on windy days rubbish was seen to be blown off as they moved slowly along. Gradually, the area was filled. The dump was on fire more often than not, and a pall of smoke usually hung over it, to the distress of the residents of Waterside and Bois Moor Road. If the fire got too bad the Fire Brigade were called to damp it down, but as it was invariably deep-seated it soon broke out again.

Flies were also a constant problem, especially in summer, when they bred profusely as there was always food among the rubbish, and seagulls also were constantly scavenging.

Gradually, over a period of some 20 years, the fill-in area extended, and was grassed over as it grew . Today, we have the large expanse of sports ground there, comprising two football and two rugby pitches – a great asset to the town's sporting facilities.

When the Moor was finally filled, our rubbish was taken to the depot at Latimer Road – where the waste disposal site is now situated. Nowadays, rubbish is all carried by large containers to a vast dump at Beaconsfield.

10. Entertainment Eighty Years Ago

I feel that the programme for *The Sleeping Beauty*, staged by Chesham Town Silver Prize Band at the Skating Rink in Red Lion Street in 1913 is worthy of reproduction. The many names involved in the production will, I am sure, stir many memories, but the amazing fact to me is '200 performers and full Orchestra'. Those of us who remember the Skating Rink will know that it was not that large a building, and however they got that number in, plus, presumably, space for an audience of some size, absolutely defies description!

Our picture of the Rink shows a poster on the front, advertising a Sale of 'Glass, China and Earthenware' by W. H. Bell. Until the 1920s, Mr. and Mrs. Bell used to visit Chesham twice a year (later, after the demise of the Skating Rink, at the Town Hall) with their wares, and stayed for about a week on each occasion.

The picture also shows the Nags Head on the left side of the road, with adjoining shops – there were antiques, sweets and butchers, together with the petrol pumps at the Nags Head garage – one of the earliest in the Town. All of these buildings were demolished when Red Lion Street was widened to allow for the increase in traffic – although I must say there was not much about when this picture was taken!

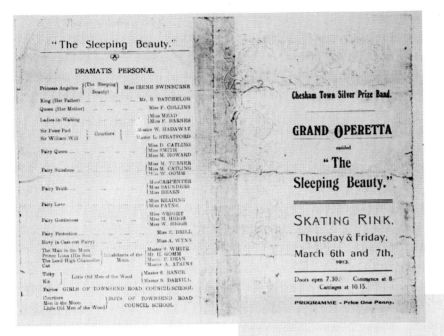

"The Sleeping Beauty."

DRAMATIS PERSONÆ.

Princess Angeline (The Sleeping Beauty)	...	Miss IRENE SWINBURNE
King (Her Father)	...	Mr. B. BATCHELOR
Queen (Her Mother)	...	Miss F. COLLINS
Ladies-in-Waiting		Miss MEAD / Miss F. BARNES
Sir Peter Peel / Sir William Will (Courtiers)		Master W. HADAWAY / Master L. STRATFORD
Fairy Queen ...		Miss D. CATLING / Miss SMITH / Miss M. HOWARD
Fairy Sunshine ...		Miss M. TURNER / Miss M. CATLING / Miss W. GOMM
Fairy Truth		Miss CARPENTER / Miss SAUNDERS / Miss HEARN
Fairy Love		Miss READING / Miss PAYNE
Fairy Gentleness		Miss WRIGHT / Miss M. HIGGS / Miss W. HIGGS
Fairy Protection		Miss E. BRILL
Envy (a Cast-out Fairy) ...		Miss A. WYNN
The Man in the Moon / Prince Luna (His Son) / The Lord High Chancellor / Cat (Inhabitants of the Moon)		Master S. WHITE / Mr. H. GOMM / Master E. DEAN / Master A. ATKINS
Ticky / Ka (Little Old Men of the Wood)		Master S. BANCE / Master S. DARVILL
Fairies	GIRLS OF TOWNSEND ROAD COUNCIL SCHOOL	
Courtiers / Men in the Moon / Little Old Men of the Wood	BOYS OF TOWNSEND ROAD COUNCIL SCHOOL	

Chesham Town Silver Prize Band.

GRAND OPERETTA

entitled

" The Sleeping Beauty."

SKATING RINK,

Thursday & Friday,

March 6th and 7th,

1913.

Doors open 7.30. Commence at 8.
Carriages at 10.15.

PROGRAMME - Price One Penny.

The Chair will be taken on
THURSDAY by
W. F. LOWNDES, Esq., J.P.

The Chair will be taken on
FRIDAY by
Rev. J. H. BROOKSBANK.

200 Performers and Full Orchestra.
Conductor - Mr. R. MOORE.

The Girls have been trained by
MISS HORSFALL,
and the Boys by MR. L. STEELE.

Costumes and Wigs ... ... Waller, Chesham.

Lighting Effects : Mr. R. J. J. Swan,
A.M.I.E.E., Engineer and
Manager, The Chesham
Electric Light and Power
Co., Ltd.

Act I.

Scene 1. A Hall in the King's Palace.
Scene 2. Room in a Cottage.

Act II.

Scene 1. The Moon.
Scene 2. A Wood.
Scene 3. As Act I, Scene 1.

A hundred years elapse between Acts I. and II.

Scenery specially prepared for this Performance.

ARGUMENT.

It is the birthday of the Princess Angeline, and isolate is being kept at the Court of the King, her father. The Fairies from the neighbouring nooks and crannies arrive to pronounce blessings on the Princess. Envy, a cast-out fairy, comes unexpectedly and pronounces her doom. According to the laws of Fairyland, "the last wish pronounced governs all the others," and Fairy Protection stipulating that Envy has come to no good purpose, cannot do herself ill. Fairy last wished, and though unable entirely to counteract her cruel words, she changes the death of the Princess to a sleep of a hundred years. And that she may not awaken alone, she causes sleep to fall on the Castle also.

Meanwhile, by the strange conduct of The Man in the Moon, preparations are going on for the fulfilment of the prophecy. Prince Luna, son of The Man in the Moon, resolves on a change at any cost, and enters the next 100 years, riding annihilation on a voyage through the air to the earth, unless thus unseen in the Moon. Happily, he arrives on the earth, and is taken in charge of the Little Old Men of the Wood, who lead him to the Sleeping Princess, and all ends in the most happiness.

The Rink will be specially heated on this occasion.

COPY OF THE PROGRAMME – ALL FOUR PAGES

13

11. The Mechanics' Institute and Literary Institute

The Mechanics – later the Literary – Institute must surely have been the earliest Men's Club to set up in the town. Early records are, I am afraid, non-existent, but the original club is believed to have been established in 1820 in an upstairs room over a shop at the rear of the Town Hall – about where Chesham Building Society offices stand today.

Late in the 1800s the club moved to an upstairs room above 11/13 High Street, and it was in these Club premises that the original Chesham Council met, following its inauguration in 1895. The usual indoor games were played: two billiard tables, later snooker, darts, chess and cards. Membership soon grew to a large number, and the club again moved to the two upstairs floors of the former Temperance Hotel at the foot of Station Road, the premises now occupied by a night club. The subscription was ten shillings a year –

quite a lot in the early years of this century. Membership reached 100, and a Library was set up. The name was then changed to the Literary Institute.

The Club never had a drinks licence – only tea, coffee, and soft drinks were available. We had a soft drinks manufacturer in the town at the time, Wallingtons of Waterside (maybe someone still has one of their old 'Cod' bottles with a marble in the top for a stopper!), so supplies were locally available. Cigarettes and confectionery were also available. The building was for years owned by International Stores, the grocery chain, and for years the Club was charged a rental of one pound a week. The late George Hawes was steward for years, and kept a close eye on the running of things. In the years following the 1914/18 War, the rent was steadily increased, and with falling membership the Club's last Treasurer, Horace Smith, found it more and more difficult to 'balance the books'. Finally, in 1934, the Club was reluctantly forced to close down. The games equipment and furniture was sold off – I understand that good Windsor chairs went for two shillings (10p) each to a local caterer. The sale realised £100, half of which was given to the Scouts and half to the Town Social Club.

12. Chesham Co-operative Society

With the local 'Co-op' now only a distant memory, I feel that a few facts concerning its century of existence should be set down. I will apologise in advance for any errors in this article, especially regarding dates, but I have found that precise information is rather hard to come by!

The local Society was set up in 1875 in the front room of a house in Church Street, when a group of like-minded residents felt that they could buy groceries wholesale and sell them more cheaply than the local small shops. Business soon prospered, and before the turn of the century the first proper shop was set up in the Broadway, opposite Broadway Baptist Church. Anyone could be a member – you joined and were allocated a membership number, which you quoted each time you made a purchase, so that your spending could be totalled up for the reckoning of your dividend. The upstairs of the building became the Equity Hall, much used for Society's events, and later to become the offices of Chesham Urban District Council.

During the first 20 years of this century, things just grew and grew, and the Society expanded into most aspects of retail trade. The original Broadway shop became both grocery and butcher's shops, and soon drapery and baker's shops were set up in the High Street, on the site now occupied by Waitrose. A large bakery was built at the rear, where all bread and cakes sold in the shops were made. No 1 Branch followed, in Berkhamsted Road at the corner of Essex Road, then came the greengrocery at 54, High Street (where Boots is now): greengrocery had previously been sold at the grocery shop. Next came hardware, when the Society took over the former Hampshire's shop at 81, High Street, then electrical, at the corner of Church Street, and, finally, in the post-war years, the furniture shop in the former Astoria Cinema (now Superdrug) in the Broadway. A further general branch was opened in Hill Avenue, Amersham. In 1933, it was decided to rationalise the business, and a fine new headquarters building was erected on the High Street site, which housed all the main departments. All the ground floor and some of the first floor were used for retail, the

SOCIETY'S TRANSPORT FLEET, BROADWAY, ABOUT 1920

GROCERY AND BUTCHERY, BROADWAY, ABOUT 1920

DRAPERS AND OUTFITTERS, HIGH STREET, 1930

16

CO-OP HALL AND
HARDWARE
SHOP, HIGH
STREET, 1930

remainder of the first floor for the Society's headquarters offices. There was a Board of Management, which met weekly to oversee the Society's affairs, and the actual day-to-day running was in the hands of a General Manager and a Secretary, later combined into a Managing Secretary.

In the early 1930s, the Society amalgamated with High Wycombe Co-operative Society, to be re-titled Chesham and Wycombe Co-operative Society. Still later, amalgamation with Tring Society came along, and their name was added to the title. Next, the name was changed to Chilterns Co-operative Society. In the post-war years the London Co-operative Society took over, and finally the Co-operative Retail Society.

With the coming of supermarkets in the 1950s and 1960s, the Society found it increasingly difficult to compete, and this, together with the relatively high cost of operation due to the fragmented nature of the business in so many different units, started the downward trend.

A dividend of 1s.6d. for every pound spent was always paid in the 1930s. This was paid out half yearly, and was always much looked forward to by members. In the post-war years this was reduced to one shilling, and finally the dividend was paid out in stamps which could be redeemed for goods in any of the Society's shops. The whole of the Society's shops finally closed down in the 1970s.

I append six pictures which I am sure will bring back memories.

In addition to the Equity Hall, mentioned above, the Society also owned the Co-op Hall at 79 High Street, and the Progress Hall above the Berkhamsted Road shop. The High Street Hall was much used for dinners,

THE FINAL DEMISE!

dances and meetings, and during the 1939/45 War years it was the local British Restaurant, where nourishing cheap meals were served. In this hall was also held the Annual Tea for elderly members, and the Annual Flower Show, also for members. I am told that the final show attracted 400 entries.

Sports facilities for employees were also provided – the Society owned two fields off Chartridge Lane, just before Berkeley Avenue – one was used for the grazing of the van horses, the other as a Sports Ground. A pavilion was erected there, and both Cricket and Football teams were run on a Thursday afternoon.

Finally, there was the Annual Co-op Fête, held on the Sports Ground on a summer Saturday afternoon; it was always a great occasion for members and their families. A fancy dress procession set off from the Berkhamsted Road shop, made its way to the Broadway, where it picked up many more, and thence proceeded up to the Field.

I am sure that there are still many memories of the 'Co-op' among older folk – it was so much a part of the town's life.

What a pity it is that, like so many other things, it faded away!

13. The Late Mr. William Lowndes

Mr William Lowndes, who lived at The Bury, Church Street, from his birth there in 1834 until his death in 1905, was truly Chesham's 'Squire'.

As a youngster he was educated privately, then went on to Trinity College, Cambridge, where he obtained B.A. and LL.B. degrees. He was called to the Bar in 1859, subsequently becoming Barrister at Law at Lincoln's Inn.

He inherited The Bury and its estates on the death of his father in 1864, and lived the life of a country gentleman in every sense of the word. He served both the Town and the County of Bucks faithfully, was a model landlord, and was ever generous to the poor and needy of the Town. On being called to the Bar he became a Commissioner of the Peace for Bucks, being regularly in attendance at the Quarter Sessions at Aylesbury. He was also a regular magistrate

THE FUNERAL PROCESSION ASCENDING THE CHURCHYARD

on the Bench at Chesham, and for a time also at Amersham. He was a member of the Local Government Board from the 1860s, and when this was superseded by the County Council he became a member of that body and served on many committees. He was later appointed Alderman.

For 40 years he was a member of the Board of Guardians of Amersham Union, being Chairman for the greater part of that time. For his services here, the Guardians presented him with a silver inkstand and with his portrait, which hung in the Boardroom of the present Amersham General Hospital for many years. He was also for years President of the local Conservative Association.

He was a devout and faithful member of St. Mary's Church, being Churchwarden for many years, and a great benefactor to the Church. He represented the Parish on the Oxford Diocesan Conference. Not only did he support his church generously, but the Nonconformist Churches in the Town also benefited from his generosity. Indeed, it was said that to each and every local institution and good cause he gave most generously.

Mr. Lowndes never married – it was said that he preferred to spend his time and money in the service of his town and county! He had extensive properties both here and in London, and also farmed locally, taking a great interest in all that he owned. He was not a great sportsman – his involvement was confined to cycling in his younger days – but he supported local sport to the full, presenting cups for competition, and his name appeared in some or other capacity in all club lists. He was an avid reader, principally of historical, legal and archeological works.

He never enjoyed robust health, and, after being ill for some years, passed quietly away at The Bury on Sunday 12 November, 1905. At Evensong at St. Mary's on that day, the Vicar (Rev. C. E. Boultbee) paid a considerable tribute to Mr. Lowndes and his life. The funeral took place in St. Mary's on 17 November, 1905, he being laid to rest in the family mausoleum in the churchyard, the last burial in that building. The event brought huge crowds to St. Mary's, the like of which had probably never been seen before – or since! Every seat in the church was filled, and hundreds stood in the churchyard. The service was conducted by the Vicar, and the hymns *'Peace perfect Peace'*, *'On the Resurrection Morning'* and *'Now the Labourer's task is O'er'* were sung.

The story goes that the route from The Bury, down to and along Church Street and up the hill to the church was thronged the entire way.

So ended an era, the like of which we shall never see again.

Many tributes to Mr. Lowndes were paid by various local organisations following his death. His hatchment bearing the family Coat of Arms with the motto, 'Ways and Means', hangs in the south transept of St. Mary's to this day.

14. Hygiene in the Home

In the 1920s and early 1930s hygiene in the home was nothing like that which we enjoy today. Most homes still had an outside lavatory, some close to the house, others at the bottom of the garden, and many shared with one or more neighbours. A few were of brick construction, but many were little wooden buildings about four feet by three feet, with a wooden seat with a round hole cut in it. Lighting was invariably by a candle, and, toilet paper being unknown to many because of its cost, the provision was a pile of cut sheets of newspaper. Whilst many of the lavatories were connected to the water supply and sewage system, there were still many earth closets where the bucket had to be emptied frequently by the Council's men, who came round with a horse-drawn vehicle bearing a tank. The smell, especially in summer, is better imagined than described.

To combat the considerable health hazard, the Urban District Council provided a free supply of disinfectant, both powder and liquid, for use by householders. This could be collected from the

Council's depot in Berkhamsted Road on a Saturday morning. Some people collected their own supplies, but many boys built up a prosperous little business by doing the collection for friends and neighbours. Most houses had two tins for powder and two bottles for liquid, so that they could be used 'one over the other'. The boy would have a two-wheeled truck, and each Saturday morning would go to the depot with one tin and one bottle for each customer. These would be filled and returned to the 'customer', and the empties collected for the following Saturday. Many boys had large trucks holding 20 or 30 'containers', and the usual 'fee' from the householder was 2d. or 3d. each week, so the boys found the work quite lucrative, and a generous addition to their pocket money, which was usually only a penny or two each week.

Another source of income for boys was the collection of rats' tails; rats were very much a problem at this time, especially in garden sheds, lavatories and also often indoors. Rat traps were standard in most homes, baited with a bit of bread and set where the rats were thought to be. When caught, the tails would be cut off and collected by a boy, who took them to the then Council Offices at 33 High Street on a Saturday morning, where they would be paid 2d. for each one. Another lucrative sideline!

DUCKS ON THE CHESS – ABOUT 1900

15. Duck Breeding

The 'Aylesbury' breed of duck, the symbol of all that is best in ducks for culinary purposes, was, of course, primarily bred in and around the town of Aylesbury, but by no means entirely. Chesham was the centre of breeding for thousands of them which were in due course sold in local shops or despatched to the London markets.

Many ducks were bred in buildings alongside the River Chess in its lower reaches, so that they could have access to the water. Hundreds could usually be seen by Chesham Moor. They were let out in the morning, and returned voluntarily at dusk to their farm which was on the site of the present Industrial Adhesives buildings. Ducklings had their own little pond (now filled in) just by the railway bridge. The noise at feeding time could be heard from far away. There were two other duck farms in Chartridge Lane until fairly recently, where again thousands were also reared, together with a number of smaller establishments around the town. Now these have sadly all gone. A fat duck for Christmas was a rare treat half a century ago, but it has now been succeeded by the all-the-year-round turkey. It is good to know that these are reared in their thousands at the farm in Chesham Vale. The only ducks now kept in the Town are the few in private gardens; in addition we do have several hundred semi-wild ones which inhabit Skottowes pond in the Park and the river alongside the Moor and Waterside.

CHESHAM TOWN BIER

22

16. The Chesham Town Bier

I append a picture of the Town Bier, which was used at the cemetery in Bellingdon Road from the opening there in 1858 and right up until its final outing in December, 1970. The original use was to carry the coffin from the horse-drawn hearse to the graveside; the hearse could only proceed to a point just inside the gates, where there was space to turn it round, and from then on the bier took over – pulled usually by one man, with another pushing, although, if the grave was at the top of the cemetery, more, of course, had to lend a hand.

It was kept in a specially built 'house' at the Bellingdon Road end of the cemetery – the house is still there – and was last used at the burial of Cemetery Superintendent William Wallington in 1970; this was felt to be appropriate as he had restored the bier in the 1960s. The 'platform' was of ash, on an iron frame which was painted black, with brass rails; the whole was mounted on iron wheels with rubber tyres. It could be used inside the cemetery free of charge; if taken outside for use at one of the town's churches there was a fee of two shillings. If taken for use outside the area of the Burial Board – the parishes of Chesham and Chartridge – the fee was four shillings. In the 1920s it was used to take the body of Miss Fanny Faithorn from her home in Germain Street (where Town Bridge Court now stands) to St. Mary's Church for the service and thence to the cemetery. Miss Faithorn, who was the daughter of much respected local Doctor George Faithorn, who died in 1871, was for years a Sunday School teacher, and the bier was pulled by four of her old pupils, Herbert Lewis, Henry Gomm, and William and Thomas Wright.

Local undertaker Arthur Stratford told the story of how, as a 14-year-old boy, he pulled the bier from its house single handedly all the way to Ashley Green Church for a funeral; he said that he puffed a bit getting it up Nashleigh Hill, which at the time was only a narrow twisting lane! Arthur also told the story of using it – his final occasion – on 4 March, 1970, when there was snow a foot deep in the cemetery; the paths had not been cleared, the hearse could not get up to the grave on the upper slopes, and the four bearers were terrified of slipping. So the faithful old bier was brought out, the coffin placed on it, and slowly pulled and pushed to its destination!

In the 1980s the bier was re-conditioned by Bob Glenister, and is now in the safe custody of the Chiltern Open Air Museum; what a pity it is that we do not yet have a museum in Chesham, the bier being so much a part of the Town's history that would surely be its rightful place!

17. Timber Carting

A familiar sight on our roads for half a century or more up until the 1930s were the horse-drawn timber carts, bringing logs – in the vast majority of instances, beech – to one of the many woodenware factories of the town. For the men involved this was a very arduous, slow and dirty occupation. There were two types of horse-drawn cart – the pole cart, which was four-wheeled, with a long strong pole between the two axles. This could be lengthened or shortened according to the length of the logs being carried. This was drawn by two horses, led – on foot – by one man. These carts usually operated in pairs, and, when they came to ascend a steep hill – all too frequent in this area – one cart would be left at the bottom whilst the four houses pulled the other to the top, leaving it there whilst they returned to drag up the second cart. On descending a steep hill, as the carts had no such things as brakes, iron shoes would be placed under the rear wheels, effectively preventing them from turning, and the horses dragged the cart down. The iron shoes invariably cut into the surface of the road, not doing it a lot of good!

These four-wheeled carts could carry several logs, depending on their size. The second type of cart was a single-axle job, carrying just one log – usually a rather large one. This was hoisted up by block and tackle to a beam above the wheels, and this was drawn by one or two horses according to the size of the log.

The carts would travel miles to fetch logs – a return journey of 8 to 10 miles could be made in a day, but far longer distances – and up to 25 or 30 miles from base was not unknown – were undertaken, the men having to find a bed for the night in a pub or lodging house. After dark, travel was not unknown, each cart carrying for illumination one lamp on each side, each powered by a candle! On arrival at a destination the horses always came first: they were taken out of the shafts, fed and watered and settled down for the night before the men thought of themselves.

On arrival at a wood to fetch the logs, which, of course, had been felled by hand, using axes and cross-cut saws – a very slow and hard job – the carts had to be loaded, again by horse power. The cart would be manoeuvred into the wood, and the logs then dragged by the horses by means of chains up to the cart. They were then dragged up two sloping poles on to the top. Most woods in winter were invariably churned up by the activities into a sea of mud, and everything soon became filthy and mud-caked – the logs, the horses and the men.

On arrival at the factory or timber yard, the logs would be unloaded by sliding them down the poles, kept in check by chains tied to the harness of the horses. No such things as cranes, of course!

By the 1930s powerful steam waggons began to replace the horse-drawn carts, then in due course motor waggons, but the horse-drawn carts did not finally fade away until well into that decade.

TIMBER CART AT CANADA WORKS

18. The Shoeing Forges and Ironworks

Throughout the ages, and until the early 1900s, the only means of transport, apart from on foot, was on horseback or by horse-drawn vehicle. For centuries, when the so-called roads were really nothing more than muddy trackways, horses could negotiate them easily, but with the coming of made-up surfaces – and these were only of flint or stone before the coming of tarmacadam – the horses' feet could not stand the wear and tear. Horseshoes were therefore early invented, and blacksmiths to make the shoes and fit them to the feet became a common sight in every town and village of any size. Chesham provided sufficient work for three blacksmiths: Wallis', originally in the Broadway, next to the present United Reformed Church, and later in Blucher Street; Goodings, in Germain Street – where Water Meadow now enters; and Ringsells, in Waterside near the railway bridge. In the forge, a blazing fire was kept going throughout the hours of work. The shoes were handmade by the blacksmith using strips of iron, which were placed in the fire until red hot, then taken out and beaten with a hammer on the anvil until they were the right size and shape, then cooled by plunging into a bucket of cold water, from which steam rose in clouds.

After removal of the old and worn shoe, the horse's foot was pared level with knife and rasp, the new shoe heated then nailed to the hoof. The noise and smell of the forge could be heard and smelt from far away, and were always a great attraction for small boys, who would gather round the always open door to have a look. Blacksmiths, of course, became very skilled men

WALLIS' FORGE, BROADWAY

GOODINGS FORGE, GERMAIN STREET

at their trade, making, in addition to horseshoes, all kinds of ironwork – gates, fences, fireplaces and wheels to name but a few. Wooden wheels of carts and carriages also were clad with an iron rim, made by the blacksmith. These wore out through constant contact with the road and had to be replaced. Many houses and gardens were surrounded by iron railings right up until the 1939/45 War, when, by Government order, they were requisitioned for making into munitions. They were ruthlessly cut down and taken to the Council Yard, where, I am sorry to say, they lay in piles for years and years as they were cast iron and of little or no use for the intended purpose!

With the coming of horse-riding as a pastime – very common in this part of the world – came the mobile farrier who attends your stable without the horse having to be taken to the forge, so our forges gradually faded away, Goodings being the last to close. The making of ironwork is today a specialised craft, and we in this area are fortunate that we have Cheelds at Hawridge, who provide a vital service to the local district.

19. Some More Gleanings from the Parish Registers

I think that the following 'snippets' may be of interest:

1. That Mr. Nathaniel Phillips Mercer of Ye Parish of St. Vedast, London, gave the sum of Two Guineas for cleaning and whitewashing this Church Anno Domini 1756.

2. Eight Church Houses built for the poor of the Parish to inhabit, situate on the South East side of the Churchyard. N.B. That the poor tenants have always been (as they are at this present) put in possession by the Minister of this Parish Presented here (by way of Memorandum) in order to preserve that Minister's prerogative. (Signed) John Ball, Vicar of Chesham, 1757. (Author's note – *The above cottages in Church Street were demolished in 1845 in order to provide the site for the Church School.*)

3. In the year of our Lord Christ One Thousand Seven Hundred and Fifty Two. Charles Lowndes Esquire having taken down the Pew belonging to his Manor House of Hundridge in this Parish and also a Pew lately purchased by him of Mrs. Miller, which heretofor belonged to her capital messuage of Pednor, the said Charles Lowndes did in the room of the said two pews build a large double pew divided by a partition in the same, and also a small pew for the use

of himself and family and as belonging to the said Manor House of Hundridge. And the said Charles Lowndes did at his own costs and charges erect a handsome screen of Wainscotwork to separate the body of the Church from the adjoining Chapel which said now double pew (together with an Isle or passage of the Church) takes up the whole space between the South East and South West Pillars of the Great Tower and between the said new erected Screen and Great Isle of the said Church. And the said small pew is situated on the North Side of the said South West Pillar. The pew belonging to the said Charles Lowndes and his family as Owner of the Capital Messuage called The Bury which Pew was formerly rebuilt by his Father William Lowndes Esquire deceased is a corner Pew on the North Side of the Great Isle and on the West side of the Middle or Cross Isle of the said Church.

In perpetual memory of which things this Entry is made and signed by us this second day of January 1753.

(Signed) John Ball Minister
Joseph Freeman Churchwardens
Edward Varney

20. Chesham Cricket Club

Although the Club is still very much alive and kicking, I feel that a few notes on its early days should be set down for posterity.

The Club was formed in 1848, and for the first 40 years of existence played at Higham Mead, off Higham Road: the site is now occupied by industry. The condition of the field was far from that of Chesham's ground today, being a bit rough and ready, as was the state of nearly all grounds at that time. In 1888 the Club obtained the use of the site of the present ground in Amy Lane, the property of Mr William Lowndes, and he generously allowed them the use at a peppercorn rent. The ground was professionally laid out, and until 1919 was used solely for cricket. Two

elevens were run, and a fairly full fixture list gradually evolved. Nearly all the local clubs featured in the list: Amersham, Berkhamsted, High Wycombe, Tring, Hemel Hempstead, Chorleywood, Northwood, Slough, Aylesbury, Luton and even Reading – some journey when it had to be made by horse drawn Waggonette. Several London clubs also featured in the list: Wembley, Paddington and Finchley. Some matches were played on a Saturday afternoon, and others on a Monday, which was apparently some sort of unofficial half day in some of our factories, particularly the boot trade. A shed was erected on the ground in which to keep the equipment, principally the horse-drawn mower, and on match days a tent was erected by Fred Lewis, known to all as 'Toby', the landlord of the Nags Head in Red Lion Street, who was long associated with the Club in many capacities. In the tent the players could change, and teas were served. The great W. G. Grace played on the ground in 1907, when he was nearing the end of his career.

In 1919, following the amalgamation of Chesham Town and Chesham General's Football Clubs into Chesham United, this Club began to use the ground. The arrangement was cricket from the third Saturday in April to the second Saturday in September, and football for the rest of the year. The Football Club brought their grandstand from the General's ground in Berkhamsted Road, and it was erected along the Amy Lane side. The Cricket Club obtained a former army hut from Halton Camp, and erected it on the site of the present pavilion. The big 'snag' was that the football pitch extended right across the cricket 'table', and when their season ended there was a tremendous amount of work necessary to get the area fit for cricket, especially after a wet winter. For some years a team of unemployed men was temporarily taken on for a couple of weeks, to get the ground in some sort of order before the opening match on the first Saturday in May. In 1929 the Chesham Sports Company was set up, and purchased the site of both the present grounds from Mr. W.F. Lowndes, who was then the owner, and in the course of a couple of years the present football ground was laid out by the Company. Football began there in September, 1932, and thereafter things became much easier for cricket; the ground was then shared only with the Cestreham Cycling and Athletic Club, who did little or no damage to the pitch.

During the 1930s the Club thrived, with two Saturday teams and a Thursday team still playing much the same fixture list. The captains in those years were, firstly, the 'Squire', Mr. W. F. Lowndes, and, later, Martin Mash, both of whom rendered invaluable service to the Club. A Cricket Week was always arranged following August Bank Holiday Monday, which was much enjoyed, particularly the fixture with a representative team from the Chesham Cricket League, always on the Thursday.

With the outbreak of war in September, 1939, many of the members soon left for military service. One team was run on a Saturday during the 1940 season,

then the Club had to close down. The pavilion was leased to the local Hebrew Community for a synagogue and school, and the ground itself was let to a farmer for the grazing of sheep. At one period during the War the Army had a tented field hospital scattered around the two grounds. With the coming of peace, members returned and soon set about re-starting things. The ground was in rather a sad state, but by dint of much hard work the first match was played in May, 1946. This season, with rather a scratch fixture list, went on and on, and, thanks to wonderful autumn weather, the final match was played in the middle of October. In the 1950s and 1960s the Club had a wonderfully prosperous period, under the successive captaincies of Jack Mash and Giffard Newton. For some years three Saturday, two Sunday, a Thursday and a Tuesday evening elevens were run, and the Club could virtually put out a team on any day of the week

W. G. GRACE
AT CHESHAM

– which they often did – to entertain touring teams. In 1962, thanks largely to the efforts of Eddie Greenham, a new pavilion was built, and opened by Freddie Trueman, to replace the 50-year-old and worn-out army hut. Bucks County matches were played there each season, and half a dozen club players received their county caps, having served with much distinction. In 1970 League cricket reached this area, and the Club had no alternative but to join in, with a much revised fixture list. A very popular Six-a-Side Tournament was run three evenings each week in June and July, well supported by many of the town's employers, and many convivial evenings took place.

It is good to know that, with ever changing conditions in sport, Chesham Cricket Club still thrives. Long may it do so.

21. Chesham Church Lads Brigade

There must still be many men – not only here in Chesham, but others living far and wide – who will remember with great affection their days in the local Church Lads Brigade Companies, both at St. Mary's and at Christ Church.

The local Companies were formed in September, 1902, the first youth organisations for boys; this was some years before the formation of the Boy Scouts. A meeting was held at White Hill School in September, 1902, following letters appearing in the *Examiner* stating that something should be done to keep the boys off the streets, and give them an interest in life, as many in the eyes of their elders, 'were a perfect nuisance and always in mischief'.

At the meeting it was agreed to form two Companies of the Church Lads Brigade – St. Mary's, meeting at the Mission Room (Emmanuel Church), under Captain W. Reynolds, and Christ Church, at Waterside Parochial Room, under Captain S. Chatterton. A Company of the Boys Brigade, at the Congregational Schoolroom, under Captain Samuel, was formed at the same meeting.

One of the first members – No. 5 on the Register – of the Christ Church Company was 13-year-old Herbert Edmunds, who transferred to the St. Mary's Company in 1908, and remained with the Brigade during the entire period of his life (Died 1959) – first as a member, then as Sergeant Instructor in 1914, Lieutenant in 1915, Captain in 1916, and remained in that rank as the Commanding Officer until handing over to his son, Leslie, who carried on as the Commanding Officer until the final disbandment of the Company in 1962. What a wonderful record of voluntary service. About a thousand boys and young men passed through the Company during its years of existence. Many – as good citizens and in addition to other voluntary activities – served the Church (many throughout their lives) as church officials, choristers, bellringers, sidesmen, lay readers etc. and several became ordained ministers of the church.

Soon after the amalgamation of the two Companies in 1908, the Brigade acquired their own headquarters in Park Road – firstly in one corrugated roofed hut, later a second for use of the band, which became such a focal and well-remembered feature of the Company. The huts were erected on land belonging to the Squire, Mr. Lowndes, who allowed the site rent-free, and in due course gave the site to the Company.

The first Commanding Officer of the Company, gazetted as Captain in 1902, was W. Reynolds, but he resigned on 1 July, 1903, on leaving for Australia for health reasons. He was succeeded by Lieutenant F. G. Brown, and the names of the initial officers and N.C.Os make interesting reading and bring back, I am sure, many memories: St. Mary's Company – Chaplain, Rev. C. E. Boultbee; Assistant Chaplain, Rev. T. A. B. Causton; Lieutenants R. W. Smith, R. G. White, G. P. Harding, W. R. Hare and A. S. Chapman; Sgt. Major G. Dover; Staff Sergeant R. Aitken; Sergeants J. Spurling and G. Pratt. Christ Church Company's first officers were Captain S. K. Chatterton; Chaplain Rev. A. E. Norman; Lieutenants R. Brocklebank, S. Lowe, A. Bates, E. Gee and C. C. Islip; Medical Officer Dr. T. F. Long, Sergeant Major

P. Elburn, Staff Sergeants F. Smith and W. Moulder, Armourer Sergeant Dan Chittenden, Orderly Room Clerk Arch Ambler; Sergeants E. Stone, H. Adams, W. Edmunds and H. Green; Corporals A. Reed, C. Power, A. Horn and C. Matthews. Many of these I am sure have descendants still living in the Town today.

The lads and officers were soon equipped with uniforms, firstly pillbox cap, belt and haversack. Rifles were added when the Company affiliated to the cadet movement; when in 1916, during World War One, it became attached to the KRR Cadet Corps, khaki uniform was adopted and continued to be worn until 1925 when they changed to blue. Funds were raised to provide instruments to form a band.

A first anniversary supper, followed by entertainment by the members, was held at Christ Church Rooms on 4 October, 1903.

The Companies met regularly, usually twice weekly, and indulged in a variety of activities: drill, physical training, rifle shooting, gymnastics and billiards. They had a regular monthly church parade when they marched to and from the Church behind the drum and fife band. The band was always a great sight, smartly turned out, well drilled and well trained, and were popular performers at many events in and around the Town in addition to Brigade events.

An annual summer camp soon became a feature; of course, very few boys ever had a holiday away from home in the early years of this century, and camp was always much looked forward to.

The first camp was in 1903 at Frensham, Surrey, and an account of the journey there at the time makes interesting reading. The two Chesham Companies marched from their respective headquarters to unite at The Pound, Red Lion Street, where they boarded, 'with Carbines and Kitbags', waggonettes for the journey to High Wycombe Station. They had, of course, to unload and walk up all hills, and it is said that the walk up Dedman Dene at Hazlemere was specially trying. At High Wycombe they caught a train to Reading Great Western Station, where they met up with other Companies of the Oxford Regiment, who were camping with them. From Reading Southern Railway Station they caught a train to Aldershot. Kit was unloaded there, and the whole regiment marched off to the camp site at Frensham Common, some seven or eight miles away. Apparently they boys kept being told 'only another mile' to keep their spirits up, and they finally arrived tired and hungry after an all-day journey which today by road would take little more than an hour. Plenty of food was provided, and spirits soon revived. A written report says that a most enjoyable camp ensued, with lots of activities. Swimming in the lakes at Frensham was very popular.

The next four years' camps were further afield – at Rottingdean, Sussex, followed by even longer journeys – to Dawlish, Seaton and Shanklin, some several times – until an abrupt end to such holidays came with the outbreak of war in 1914. The older members of the Brigade, together with many past members, immediately volunteered for service in the Army, and the C.L.B. in this region formed the 16th Battalion, Kings Royal Rifle Corps, later also the 19th Battalion. The 16th were mustered at Denham prior to

PHOTO OF REUNION DINNER

going to France, where they fought with great distinction and suffered many casualties. Almost 30 local lads lost their lives there. Their record of awards speaks for itself: during the whole conflict the 16th (CLB) Battalion KRR's won: 2 D.S.O.s; 26 M.C.s; 3 D.C.s; 130 M.M.s; and 2 Croix de Guerre.

A great sense of fellowship developed with the people of Denham before going to France, and they really won the hearts of the villagers. So much so that, after the War, the survivors organised a reunion, with parade service and lunch there. This continued every year right up until the 1970s, by which time numbers had grown small with the passing of the years.

In spite of the loss of so many members, Herbert Edmunds, who had been rejected for service on medical grounds, set about rebuilding the Company in 1915 with younger boys. Travel was difficult, but a camp was held at Latimer in 1915, in 1916 and 1917 at The Lee, in 1918 at Witney, and in 1919 at Marlow. Thereafter, the pattern of visits to seaside camp sites resumed, and this continued until war once again broke out in 1939. During this war camps were held fairly locally, mainly at Marlow, where the lads were able to help farmers with the harvest. On the return of peace the normal pattern resumed, Captain Edmunds by this time being ably assisted by his sons, Ray and Les. Ray had served six years as Sergeant in the local Home Guard and Les had served for six years in the Royal Engineers. Both became Lieutenants in the Company. Thus the Company continued, I am afraid now with falling numbers, as so many other activities became available for boys, and the Company sadly closed down in 1962.

A Golden Jubilee Reunion was held in Chesham on 19 October, 1952, attended by many past and present members of the Company, including Capt. Brown, Commanding Officer from 1903 to 1914. A commemorative service was held in St. Mary's followed by a great supper for 200 in the Church Rooms. This was an evening of great memories, when many old comradeships were renewed and tales of past events re-told.

22. Our Former Laundries

I imagine that I am correct in saying that, in the 1990s, the majority of homes possess an automatic washing machine, which over the past twenty years has become almost a necessity! Those who do not possess a machine have the use of our local launderette, at the corner of Queens Road.

Before the advent of such machines, washing of clothes was either done at home or by sending them to the local laundry. For many years we had the choice of two, the Royal Bucks in Waterside and the Perfection in Eskdale Avenue. Both, of course, have now long since disappeared, but I am sure that there are still many in the Town who have memories of them – either as a customer, or, especially among the ladies, as an employee, as the staff, apart from a handful of men who were the engineers or van drivers, were entirely female.

The Royal Bucks was set up around the turn of the century in the former silk mill, which had for almost half a century provided employment in the weaving of silk and velvet – another of Chesham's long-forgotten trades. This laundry was owned and run by the Jackson family, of whom John and Fred will long be remembered, as employees, as cricketers for Chesham, and Fred especially as a stalwart of the local British Legion. Clothes were collected on a regular weekly basis by one of the fleet of vans which were a regular sight in the district in their blue livery with the Dutch Girl logo on the side. Your clothes were returned a few days later, washed, ironed, or immaculately pressed as necessary. In the 1930s, when the Royal Bucks was in its heyday, an office block and a house for the manager were erected on the Waterside frontage. The Perfection Laundry was in Eskdale Avenue – a block of flats now stands on the site – and, though being the smaller of the two, gave an equally good service.

Washing machines and launderettes began to appear in the 1960s, which, of course, began to have a detrimental effect. Perfection was the first to succumb in the late 1960s, and in the 1970s the Royal Bucks too

*ROYAL BUCKS
LAUNDRY*

*SOCIAL
GATHERING AT
ROYAL BUCKS
LAUNDRY*

closed down, there being insufficient trade to survive. It was demolished, together with the houses in Gordon Road which ran alongside, and was replaced by large blocks of Local Authority housing, which provides homes for many.

During the years of the 1939/45 War, and for a few years after, the large club room on the first floor of the Royal Bucks was regularly used for dances. I think that the admission was one shilling. Many will surely remember these, especially during the years of 1942/45 when the United States Air Force was stationed at Bovingdon, and many of their men came down to the dances much to the delight of the local young ladies! In the post-war years a well-known local dance band, Alan Clark and his Music, regularly played there, and will I am sure be remembered with affection. Finally, the room was declared unsafe – there was a horrid prospect of both floor and dancers collapsing into the works below. So yet another of Chesham's much-loved entertainment venues disappeared. Happy memories for many I am sure!

23. Cestreham Cycling and Athletic Club

The Club was formed around the year 1900, its aim being to give 'Good Healthy Recreation' to the young men of the town and district. This was the time when people were really beginning to take an interest in sport. Working hours in the local factories were a bit shorter than they had been ever since the Industrial Revolution – a half-day (from 1 p.m.) on Saturday (instead of from 4 p.m.), and weekday hours were now usually from 8 a.m. to 6 p.m., so on summer evenings and at weekends the young men were glad of recreation.

The Club was the idea of a group of local business men, with the ever-interested Squire Lowndes as President, and many other well-known names as Patrons. Headquarters were at the Crown Hotel, Market Square, which had several meeting rooms in the yard at the rear. What a pity this well-known hostelry was ever allowed to be demolished in the 1950s to become a supermarket. What an asset to the Town it would be today, when we have not a single hotel in which to hold a dinner or reception!

By arrangement with the Cricket and Football Clubs, which both used the present cricket ground until 1932, the newly-formed Club was permitted to mark out an oval track around the outside of the cricket square – I believe that it was six laps to the mile – and were allowed to use the pavilion on one or two evenings a week during the summer months. The athletics section practised both short and long distance races, and the cycling section used the same track, although most of that section's racing was done on the open road – far fewer cars on the road than there are today. There was a good deal of inter-club rivalry, and every club held an open meeting at least once a year.

Cestreham's annual meeting was invariably on the Tuesday following August Bank Holiday Monday, and was always a great day in the town. The first meeting was in 1902, and these continued until the 1930s, when the Cricket Club instituted a Cricket Week with matches every day following Bank Holiday, so the Cestreham could no longer have use of the ground.

Clubs from all around the area – as far as Reading, Chelmsford and all parts of London – sent competitors, and for some years a special train was laid on from Marylebone to bring down competitors and their supporters. Racing – both athletic and cycling – was continuous from 2 to 7 p.m., when the prizes were presented by a local dignitary – often Mrs. H. A. V. Byrne, the wife of the Managing Director of Chesham Brewery, a man involved with most organisations in the Town – who lived at 'The Cottage', next door to the cricket ground. Prizes were remarkably generous for the period: a number of both athletic and cycling events had prizes of £5, £2 and £1. When one considers that a man earning £2 a week was considered very well off – well . . . ! Following prizegiving, an enclosure was set aside for dancing to the music of Chesham Silver Prize Band. The

admission for this was threepence.

The cycling section, in addition to activities in the Town, had a regular programme of outings: a local run on summer evenings, and a full day out on many Sundays of the year – often to the South Coast, sometimes as far as Devon (a two-day event) and also to the Cotswolds and other places of interest in the Midlands – anything up to 200 miles in a day.

The Club held its annual dinner at the Oak Room of the Crown Hotel. It survived in a small way throughout the 1914/18 War, and in the early 1920s became strong again. The 1939/45 War again caused a decline, and on the resumption of peace the use of the cricket ground was lost. For some years the Club continued to operate on the Lower Moor, and the athletics section always took part in the track events at the Annual Whit Monday Fete, which was for some years until the 1960s a joint venture by the Cricket and Football Clubs, held on the Football Ground. This always drew a large crowd and made a lot of money for the two clubs. This event – like the Cestreham Club's – finally faded away in the 1960s: two more Chesham institutions gone – what a pity!

24. The Town's Slaughterhouses

Today, as we see consignments of frozen meat arriving at our supermarkets and butchers' shops, I am sure that few of us give a thought as to where the carcasses originated, or where they were slaughtered and frozen. Until the 1930s refrigeration and deep freezing were almost unknown and all meat was sold fresh.

Chesham boasted four slaughterhouses, where the

locally raised cattle, sheep and pigs were slaughtered and prepared ready for sale. These were at Broad Street (Aitken's, which stood at the rear of the butcher's shop of that name, situated just about where St. Mary's Way now commences); High Street (where the Broadway Newsagent's shop now stands); a second farther down the High Street (at the rear of Clay's the butchers, which was just about where Lunn Poly now stands); and Blucher Street (the Co-op's building, now totally disappeared). It was a common sight on several mornings each week to see beasts being driven from their farms through the streets to their respective destinations.

There was always much noise and shouting from the drovers, as the entrances to all the slaughterhouses were quite narrow and the beasts were reluctant to enter, perhaps sensing their coming fate. I am sure that the methods used (the noise emanating during the slaughter was blood-curdling) and the standards of hygiene at the time would hardly meet today's E.E.C. standards, but such was the system prevailing at the time.

As stated above, all meat was sold fresh, and many of our poorer folk waited until just before the 7 p.m. closing time on a Saturday to purchase their Sunday joint, as prices were invariably reduced by then, especially in warm weather, when the meat would probably have 'gone off' by Monday morning.

25. Our Drainage System

Our original main drainage – or sewer – system was laid down in the late 1800s, and by the 1930s, with the enormous growth of the town, especially at the northern end, it had become woefully inadequate. The pipes were of earthenware, and were leaking badly into the subsoil. Our Council, therefore, decided that a complete renewal of the 'main line' through the town was essential, incorporating the recently introduced cast iron pipes. The traffic on the roads at the time was nothing like that of today, but it was still a problem. The work along Broad Street was carried out without too much disruption, but when it came to the High Street it was a different matter. The sewer line was right in the middle of the road, which had to be closed. But how? There was no Backs, East Street, or St. Mary's Way; High Street was the only road through the town centre. Traffic was, therefore, diverted via Bellingdon Road or Blucher Street to the Park, along

The Avenue, down Bury Lane, into Church Street and out to the Market Square. The Park avenue was just about wide enough for two vehicles to pass, including the double decker buses which had recently been introduced on the Amersham, High Wycombe and Windsor routes, but Bury Lane was a different matter. It had a 90-degree turn at both ends, so a one-way system had to be set up. Electric signalling had not at the time been though of, so 'Stop' and 'Go' boards, each operated by a man, were set up at both the Park

RE-LAYING THE SURFACE OF HIGH STREET, 1930

and Church Street ends. These had to be operated 24 hours a day, with red and green oil lamps used during the hours of darkness. Hold-ups were frequent, with many troubles caused by buses and lorries in narrow Church Street. The work on the sewer was slow and lasted for many weeks, due to the waterlogged nature of the subsoil; pumps were constantly in use, discharging water into High Street, which was a thoroughly messy place for both shoppers and shopkeepers. Still, the town kept going!

In 1935 it was decided to re-lay the surface of the lower High Street from Station Road to Church Street, with the newly invented wood block roadway. Again, the traffic had to be diverted through the Park; the volume had grown by this time, and even more hold-ups occurred.

The existing tarmacked surface was dug up and excavated to a depth of some 18 inches, and the spoil carted away – many loads of it. A thick bed of concrete was then laid down, and, when dry, the wooden blocks, some six-inches thick, were carefully laid over the top. The surface was then coated with tar. This new system did not prove a great success; all too soon, as usual, one of the public utility companies needed to excavate to work on their various pipes, and excavation was a difficult and costly job. In addition, the blocks wore rather unevenly and depressions appeared. The system had to last throughout the years of the 1939/45 War, but early in the post-war period the whole surface was dug up and removed, and the now-popular tarmacadam surface was laid, which lasted until the street was again dug up for pedestrianisation a few years ago.

26. Bois Moor Road – Water Supply

Until 1934 the whole of the Bois Moor Road area, together with Woodley Hill, was outside the boundaries of Chesham. The area was, and always had been, in the civil parish of Chesham Bois. This was in the Amersham Rural District Council's area, and at the time had little in the way of public services; the principal ones lacking were a piped water supply and a sewage system. Your water was obtained from one of the three 'water holes' which were spread alongside the road in the watercress beds. Each hole was fenced off and was about a yard square, edged by stone blocks. The water was about a foot deep. Access was down three or four stone steps. The water in the holes was clear and spring-like, although totally untreated in the way that our water supplies are today. The residents of the area had to take their buckets to the holes for every drop of water required, and on a Monday morning – the universal wash day – the water carriers were a constant procession. What a chore!

Similarly, there was no such thing as a flush toilet in the area. Most houses had a 'privy' – sometimes to themselves, sometimes shared with others – either attached to the house or at the top of the garden, usually a shed-like structure made of wood or corrugated iron, about a yard square. The bucket in there had to be frequently emptied and the contents disposed of. There was a fairly regular collection service, but many householders preferred to use a hole dug in the garden. It was always said that the gardens in this area grew the biggest and finest cabbages in the town; I wonder why?

On 1 April, 1934 – only just over 60 years ago, and well within the memory of many – the boundaries of Chesham Urban District were greatly enlarged by almost three times and took in large parts of the Parishes of Chesham Bois, Latimer, Ashley Green, Hawridge and Chartridge, and Bois Moor Road became just another road in the town. The usual, and very necessary, public services were soon provided there.

Today, as we turn on the tap or flush the toilet, we give not a thought to the matter; but just think what it would be like without them, and what our ancestors had to endure.

In spite of the rather primitive conditions which prevailed in the area above, I do not think that an epidemic of any serious disease ever occurred.

Perhaps it speaks well for the hardness and purity of Chesham's water, which persists to this day. I am sure that many of us have had a drink of water when on holiday in other parts, and have said, 'Oh, give me a drink of Chesham's *real* water any day!' I know that I have.

27. The Isolation Hospital

For centuries the population was plagued with periodic outbreaks of infectious diseases – diphtheria, typhoid, smallpox and scarlet fever among the most prevalent – and the mortality rate among sufferers was very high. Due to their infectious nature, the diseases were often spread rapidly to other members of the family, and also to friends and neighbours who came to the house to help, as was usually the custom at that time. There was no such thing as inoculation against such diseases.

Our first attempt to isolate and care for such sufferers was the provision by the Local Board (the predecessor of the Urban District Council) of the Pest House. This was in Bellingdon Road (where Deansway now enters). Indeed, the road there was known as Pest House Lane. Patients were kept there under somewhat primitive conditions with little or no nursing as we know it today, during the period of infection. If you recovered, so be it; I am afraid that many did not. The Pest House survived until 1902, when Chesham Urban District Council built and opened the 'Infectious Hospital' along Chesham Vale – just beyond where the Brown's agricultural machinery depot stands today, the old Pest House then being converted into cottages, which survived until the 1930s. The new hospital was built outside Chesham's boundary, in the Rural District Council's area, and it is said that that body were never very happy with it. It was opened only when there was an epidemic – the Council did not want to pay staff when there was nothing to do – so, of course, the staff were somewhat casual – they were not paid when the hospital was closed. The building was of corrugated iron sheeting on a wooden frame, and was painted red – just the colour for a hospital! This hospital in turn survived until the 1930s, when a proper isolation hospital was opened at Aylesbury, and Chesham's cases were treated there. The building was then converted into two dwellings, which provided two homes until after the 1939/45 War. It then became more and more derelict, and was finally demolished in the 1960s, when two modern bungalows were erected on the site.

28. Peace Celebrations – 1919

The day of peace celebrations in August, 1919, following the end of the Great War, must have been one of the most all-embracing days in our long history. Events commenced with an enormous grand carnival procession, which left Brockhurst Road at 10 a.m. and proceeded right through the Town, down Germain Street, King Street and Amy Lane to Bois Moor, then returned to the Broadway via Waterside and Red Lion Street. Chesham Town Silver Prize Band naturally had the honour of leading, followed by a large contingent of ex-service men, Girl Guides, Football and Cricket Clubs, decorated cycles, Red Cross workers, decorated prams, Friendly Societies, Boy Scouts band, Church Lads' Brigade, fancy costumes, tableaux, decorated trade carts, decorated motor cycles and cars, and the First Hendon Boy Scouts, in that order.

At 1 p.m., there was a great lunch party for all ex-service men, those still serving, and dependents of the fallen. The numbers were so large that the lunch had to be held at two venues – at Germain Street School, where Fred Lewis of the Nags Head was the caterer, and at the Church Rooms, Church Street, where Mr. Nind of Chartridge was the caterer. Food and drink were plentiful at both venues.

Following lunch, there was a great sports meeting at the Top Park (where Chesham Park Community College now stands), comprising no fewer than 21 events for all ages from the under-sevens to ex-service men and the disabled (who had a special 30-yards flat

*PIGEON FANCIERS'
FLOAT*

*PLANTING OF THE
VICTORY OAKS*

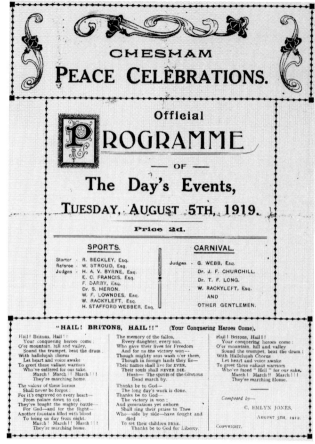

CHESHAM
PEACE CELEBRATIONS.

Official
PROGRAMME
— OF —
The Day's Events,
TUESDAY, AUGUST 5TH, 1919.

Price 2d.

SPORTS.	CARNIVAL.
Starter R. BECKLEY, Esq.	Judges G. WEBB, Esq.
Referee W. STROUD, Esq.	Dr. J. F. CHURCHILL.
Judges H. A. V. BYRNE, Esq.	Dr. T. F. LONG.
E. C. FRANCIS, Esq.	W. RACKYLEFT, Esq.
F. DARBY, Esq.	AND
Dr. S. HERON.	OTHER GENTLEMEN.
W. F. LOWNDES, Esq.	
W. RACKYLEFT, Esq.	
H. STAFFORD WEBBER, Esq.	

"HAIL! BRITONS, HAIL!!" (Your Conquering Heroes Come).

PROGRAMME FOR THE GREAT DAY

race), and veterans over 50. Lady Chesham presented some 70 prizes following the meeting.

At 4 p.m. there was a great open air tea for all children between 5 and 15. This was followed by two grand variety entertainments on the same site, at 5 and 7.30 p.m., comprising clowns, contortionist, marionettes, comedians and singers – all professionals. Seats for this (wooden chairs) were provided at sixpence or a shilling. At the same time, there were Punch and Judy shows for children given

by Mr. W. J. Pearce (I am sure he is still remembered with affection by many older folks).

From 7 to 9.30 p.m. there was dancing on the Cricket Ground at the top of the Park (this was the Social Club's ground), music being provided, of course, by the Town Band. Open air dancing was a very popular event on summer evenings at this period – and, indeed, well into the 1930s – very pleasant it was too on a warm evening. What a pity it has now almost completely died out.

The great day finally ended with a grand display of fireworks in the Top Park.

The *Bucks Examiner*, on 8 August, in reporting the day very fully, stated: 'Until nearly midnight some thousands (remember Chesham's population was only 8,000 then) tasted the open air life to the full – fortune it was that the Park had been chosen – healthy and open, broad and free – the people swarmed up there and spent a joyous time.'

During the afternoon, the Victory Oaks had been planted in the Park – they are still there, between the Girl Guide hut and the bowling green. The first was planted by Lady Chesham and Major Lionel de Rothschild, M.P., and the second by Mr. and Mrs. W.F. Lowndes and Mr. and Mrs. H.A.V. Byrne.

There were also representatives of the Allies present – Madame Chaumette (France), Madame Del Monaco (Italy), Lady Swettenham (America), Father Flanagan (Ireland) a lady representing Poland and Rev. P. V. Boyes for the Motherland and Colonies. Mr. Frank Howard acted as M.C. What a gathering of personalities!

It was not until two years later, on Sunday, 24 July, 1921, that our War Memorial in the Broadway was unveiled and dedicated. There had earlier been a temporary memorial in the Market Square. In the Broadway there was a service of dedication conducted by the Vicar, Rev. C. E. Boultbee, and, after giving an address, the Marquis of Lincolnshire, who was Lord Lieutenant of Bucks, unveiled the memorial. The Last Post was sounded, followed by Reveille, and the event closed with the National Anthem.

29. Chesham's Last Town Crier

Many of our older residents will remember the Town's last Town Crier, Philip Howard, who was a great character in the Town in the 1920s and 1930s.

Philip was a member of a very well-known and prosperous local family, but, like many others both before and since, chose to 'cast adrift' and do his own thing. As a young man he was a great athlete, and our picture shows him – centre – outside The Cock with two other well-known personages – Archie Moore (left – baker) and George Eldridge (right – slaughterman).

Philip lived for years in a cottage off Duck Alley, Germain Street, and in addition to being Town Crier he was 'general factotum' of Chesham's market, at that time held in the Market Square (dare I say where it should be now!). He kept the stalls (portable wooden affairs) in the lower part of the Town Hall. They would be erected on a Thursday evening in readiness for Friday's market, following which they would be left in position for Saturday. This day's market lasted until 8 or 9 p.m., many people waiting until nearly that hour to purchase their meat and fish. It was always reduced in price as the evening wore on in pre-refrigeration days. After closure Philip would dismantle and pack away the stalls, finally sweeping up the considerable amount of rubbish which was always left.

As Town Crier Philip would 'cry' – or announce – literally anything that was required, but his chief duty seemed to be to announce that the water supply was about to be turned off. He would walk around the area concerned, ringing his handbell (which is still preserved in the Town Council Offices) at every street corner and crying in a loud voice, 'O Yea! O Yea! O Yea! This is to give notice the water will be turned off from half past one till three.' (This was invariably the period.) This was so that, in the days before tanks in the roof, the housewife could fill her kettle and buckets for use during the 'No Water' period. Philip also 'cried' to announce fêtes and any other event of interest; I believe that his payment for each job was one shilling.

On the demolition of Duck Alley in the 1930s under Chesham Council's Slum Clearance programme, Philip, ever the independent, moved to a caravan (a self converted Royal Bucks Laundry van) in a field at the top of Trapps Lane (where Rose Drive now stands). What he did for the 'usual services' no-one ever knew, but he survived there until his death in the 1940s.

PHILIP HOWARD (CENTRE)

30. The Golden Ball – Chesham's Farmers' Pub

For several centuries, until its closure some ten years ago, the Golden Ball in Church Street was not only a public house but also the meeting place for many of the farmers of the district, who not only had a drink there on their visits into the Town, but also conducted much of their business there. I suppose that much of the reason for this – in the present century at least – was the character of the man who was landlord there for 55 years – the late Harry Wing, who was surely one of the best-known men in the district.

The house was, for over a century, the property of Wellers, the great Amersham brewing company, who owned and supplied over 50 pubs in this part of Bucks,

in parts of Herts and also in Middlesex. When the Weller business was sold in 1929, it became part of the Benskins Company, and so remained until its eventual closure some ten years ago.

Harry Wing came to Chesham in 1905 from Radlett, and took over the house in that year as a young man of 24. He held the licence continuously until 1960, when, approaching his 80th year, he retired to Broadview Farm on the northern outskirts of the Town. In the early years of his tenancy the house was also the office of the local Excise Officer, who spent much of his time measuring the strength of the beer being brewed at Chesham Brewery..

Harry, in addition to being publican, became a licensed horse slaughterer. This was not for the slaughter of animals for human consumption, but for animals which were old, diseased or injured. Some were brought to the yard for slaughter, but the vast majority were dealt with at the farms or stables where they were kept – over a wide area, up to 30 miles away. He would turn out on literally any day of the year when the call came, driven in his lorry by his faithful driver; he himself never learned to drive. Following slaughter, the animal was hoisted on to the lorry by a hand winch – no easy job with a large bull or cart horse. The carcass was then brought back to the yard for dismemberment. All types were dealt with: horses, cattle, sheep and pigs. Harry held an official slaughterer's licence from Chesham Urban District Council for over 60 years. In the yard the beasts were cut up and sold for pet food – this, of course, long before the days of tinned petfoods. A lump of meat costing sixpence or a shilling, when boiled, would feed a dog or cat for a week at least, and people came from all over the district to buy their supplies. Consignments were regularly sent to the kennels of the Old Berkeley Hunt at Amersham, for the hounds, and during the 1939/45 War, when Bertram Mills Circus was based for the duration at Chalfont St. Giles, they too purchased meat for the animals.

Mr. Wing paid a few shillings or pounds – depending on the size – to the farmer for each animal.

The trade was not always constant; sometimes there was a shortage, sometimes a glut; when the latter happened it was sold to a company called Harrison Barber, who had their premises in London.

Harry not only slaughtered animals: in many cases he cured them of their disease! Never trained as a vet., he nevertheless assimilated a vast knowledge of animals and their diseases, and would often tell the farmer just what to do to put the animal right. For this, he was much respected among the farming community.

Another sideline was dealing in horses. Let us remember that, at the time, the chief means of motivation was the horse. Harry knew through his constant contact with the farmers when they would be needing a new animal, and would in due time cross over to Ireland to purchase a consignment. He had a good eye for a good animal, and following purchase in Limerick would arrange for them to be shipped over to Fishguard, from whence they would be sent by rail to Berkhamsted Station. On unloading, they would be walked to their respective new homes, often ten miles or more away. In this trade Harry always had the reputation of being a true and fair dealer.

"TRANSPORT TO THE STATION FOR THE PIGEONS"

44

The upstairs room at the pub was for years used as the meeting place of the local branch of the National Farmers Union, and at these meetings much buying and selling of both livestock and implements also took place. On Saturday evenings the farmers gathered in the bar for their weekly 'Night Out' with a few (or more) drinks, and there is a true story regarding one man who lived several miles out of the town and who came in by horse and trap. He invariably partook of rather too much, and at closing time he would be manhandled on to the trap by his pals, the reins would be put in his hands, and the horse would be told to 'Go Home'. The trap was lit by just two candle lamps, but the horse never failed; it, the trap and the boss were always safely delivered. You cannot do that with motor vehicles.

Another organisation which used the Golden Ball for years was the local Pigeon Racing Club. The birds – in their respective baskets – would be brought to the Yard on a Friday evening during the racing season, and then taken by horse and cart to the Station for despatch to their release point – invariably several hundred miles away. The racing clocks would be kept at the yard. On Saturday morning the birds would be released for their flight home, where the owner would be anxiously awaiting their arrival. Once the bird had entered its loft and could be caught, the ring on its leg would be removed and conveyed as fast as possible, usually by bicycle, to the yard, where it would be put through the clock to record its time of arrival. The winning pigeon could be determined when all birds were home and recorded.

The Old Berkeley Hunt always met once a year at the Golden Ball, and the event was a great spectacle – crowds always gathered around the area to see the 'Off', and this meet always attracted a large field of riders and followers.

The Master at this time was Mr. Stanley Barratt, of Kings Langley, and many of the local 'gentry' were among the riders. After giving up the licence on retirement in 1960, Harry continued the slaughterhouse business for a few more years, until it closed down. The pub itself was closed down and converted into offices in the 1980s, and is now a doctor's surgery – renamed 'Aureole House'. At least the 'Golden' connection is still there!

Harry's son, (also Harry) still lives and farms in Chesham, but has never entered the licensed or slaughterhouse trade; his daughter, Sheila, is also still living locally.

OLD-WORLD SETTING FOR OLD BERKLEY HUNT MEET.

The Ancient Church Street Cottages, with the Parish Church in the Background.

OLD BERKELEY HUNT AT THE GOLDEN BALL – 1933

31. The Hospital Carnival

In the days prior to the coming of the National Health Service in 1948, our Cottage Hospital, like the great majority of other hospitals in this country, had to be self-supporting financially. Many residents belonged to the 'penny a week' scheme – where collectors called on their local members and on factories to collect a weekly contribution of a penny or twopence from each person, which scheme in total raised quite a lot of money each year. In addition to this, there was a great hospital fête in the grounds of The Bury on the last

Thursday of July each year, when the town virtually closed down for the afternoon so that everyone could take part.

Then there was Hospital Carnival Saturday, always held in September, and always a great occasion in the town. The many decorated floats would be carefully planned long in advance, and surreptitious enquiries made to see what other organisations were doing so that yours did not clash. Arrangements were made to borrow a horse and cart or other vehicle, and the construction of the float was always a matter of much thought. Decoration would usually be done on the previous Friday evening, in a factory or public house yard. The embryonic procession would gradually assemble on the Saturday morning in Brockhurst Road, where the last-minute touches always had to be put. The procession would move off in the afternoon, traversing the entire length of the town before dispersal. Collecting tins were always rattled along the entire route, and several hundred pounds were invariably collected, a lot of money in the 1920s.

The Carnival was held from the early 1920s until the mid-1930s, when, due to two things, the ever-increasing motor traffic through the town which did not take kindly to a considerable hold-up whilst the procession wended its slow way through the streets, and diminishing enthusiasm among the entrants, it unfortunately faded away. Fortunately, we now have the Schools of Chesham Carnival every June, which has resurrected the tradition.

I append four pictures taken in various years; I feel sure that they will re-kindle memories among our older residents.

32. Great Days of Chesham United Football Club

A dinner was held at the Town Hall on 30 May, 1922, to celebrate what must have been the Club's best ever season – 1921/22. During that season the Club won the following:

Berks and Bucks Cup
Bucks Charity Cup
Chesham Charity Cup
Spartan League, Divisions 1 and 2
Chesham and District League, Division 1

I am pleased to quote from the Souvenir Brochure which was printed for the occasion:

A Dip into History

'For an infant born on December 1st, 1917, Chesham United is a very sturdy and lusty youngster. In a way that was to be expected, for it has a notable parentage, its sire being Chesham Town, born in 1879, and its dam, Chesham Generals, born in 1887. At this notable time in its career, it is interesting to glance at history. In 1917, when football was officially "dead", those two fine sportsmen, Mr. William Darvell and Mr. Percy Dormer, conceived the idea that then was a favourable opportunity to once more (the idea had been previously put forward without success) propose the amalgamation of Chesham Town and Chesham Generals. They each approached a select few; the idea caught on; an Advisory Committee was appointed; the Committee consulted amicably; the work bore fruit; the Chesham United Football Club was born on December 1st, 1917. The successful Committee was: The late Mr. H. A. V. Byrne, who acted as Chairman; Dr. T. F. Long; and Messrs. R. Beckley, J. G. Stone, H. Smith, F. J. Wilson, W. Hawes, A. T. Stephenson, J. Herbert (the late), P. C. Dormer (the late) and W. Darvell (Hon. Secretary). Mr. J. G. Stone, who has for forty-three years been connected with local Football, was appointed Hon. Secretary, Mr. F. J. Wilson, for long the valued Treasurer of Chesham Generals, the Hon. Treasurer. Mr. H. A. V. Byrne was appointed neutral Chairman, and the Committee was a blending of each of the old Committees – six from each, as follows: from Chesham Generals – Messrs. W. Hawes, H. Lacey, E. Hunnibell, W. White, C. Webb and W. J. Humphrey; Chesham Town – Messrs. R. Beckley, W. Holliman, H. Smith, J. Wood, F. Keen and G. Darvell. There have only been three changes since: Mr. Byrne (deceased), Mr. Humphrey and Mr. Stephenson (who took Mr. Humphrey's place) leaving the Committee, and on his retirement Mr. Albert Moulder was appointed; while Mr. G. H. Barnes went on the Committee as Captain of the First Eleven. To ensure continuity of policy the Committee was appointed to hold office until "the first day of August in the third year following the re-commencement of official football" and that term expires on August 1st this year.

The colours adopted were Claret and Blue; the ground chosen Chesham Sports Ground, generally known as Chesham Cricket Ground.

One Cup Year

The first Season, 1919/20, will not soon be forgotten. Chesham entered the Spartan and Great Western Suburban Leagues. The League performances were negligible: fifth in the Spartan League (Played 20; Won 11; Drew 2; Lost 7. Goals 58 – 46, Points 24) – and eighth in the Great Western Suburban League. But the Cup performances – especially the Amateur Cup – were memorable, despite many Away matches. In the Amateur Cup Uxbridge and Wealdstone were beaten 8 – 0 and 4 – 2 at Chesham; Yiewsley 5 – 1 Away; Hampstead 2 – 1 Away (Divisional Final); Aylesbury 2 – 0 at Chesham, and Bromley Away 0 – 5. Up to the time they visited Hampstead, Chesham were undefeated, and at Hampstead they succeeded where Wycombe failed. The best F.A. Cup performance was at Dunstable, where Luton Clarence were beaten by 3 – 0. The Cup team was C. Webb; H. Redding and W. Brandon; Bert Sawyer, A. Gomm and L. T. Stillman; A. Wright, E. Carter, W. Keen, Geo. H. Barnes and W. Vine. Cyril Webb was Captain. W. Keen that Season left Chesham for Millwall, after being the mainstay of the attack.

Of the Season 1920/21 little need be said. In the Spartan League Chesham finished third in both Divisions, and that Season Wycombe Wanderers secured the championship of each Division.

The Brave Six

The Season we are now celebrating (1921/22), – the third Season, the second of George H. Barnes Captaincy – has established a record for all time for the Town and the County, if not for the Country. Six trophies grace our Board. Not since 1908 has the County Cup come to Chesham, and then Chesham Town beat Windsor and Eton by 2 – 0; this time well beat Wycombe Wanderers by 2 – 0 in a replay. Not since 1913/14 had the League Championship come to Chesham; then Chesham Generals secured that honour, and made up a trio, winning also the Bucks Charity and Chesham Charity cups. The significant thing was that we beat every Club of note in Berks and Bucks whom we met, and the one Club we did not meet was Maidenhead: and we beat Middlesex and Herts Representatives. The finish of the Season, when Chesham First Eleven was called upon to perform superhuman tasks, and succeeded in spite of the heavy work, will live in memory. The successful Cup and League team was A. C. Taylor; W. Brandon and F. Pearson; H. Dean, A. Gomm and L. T. Stillman; R. Garton, H. Perkins, R. Lacey, A. W. Oakes, and Geo. H. Barnes (Captain). One of the youngest Forward lines ever put out. Last Season Ron Garton was playing for his school side, and scored 51 goals in 11 matches; this Season he has played for a Senior side, and won four medals. The performances speak for themselves; the large scoring; the small number of goals against, and the fine goal average are all hard facts. The Second Eleven have had a good Season under the Captaincy of Cyril Webb, and their record speaks for itself. The chief players have been C. Webb; H. Redding; S. Ringsell; F. Newman: G. Hammond: A. Wright; Chris. Rance; M. Barnes; E. Woodford; J.

Rogers; F. Filby and Sid Rance.

Just a few figures

Statistics are a bore, but these few figures speak eloquently:-

First Eleven. Played 44; Won 31; Drawn 4; Lost 9. Goals 169 for; 49 against.
Second Eleven. Played 42; Won 31; Drawn 5; Lost 6. Goals 183 for; 60 against.
On the mark!!

Several of our forwards have been decidedly "on the mark"; considering the comparatively small number of matches he played in, Corporal A.W. Oakes had a valuable tally of goals. H. Perkins, our good recruit from Sutton Court, heads the First Eleven list and nearly but not quite reached his half century.

County Men.

The quality of the men we possess is borne out by the fact that a large number of the team are county players: G. H. Barnes, L. T. Stillman, W. Brandon, H. Dean, A. Gomm and A. C. Taylor.

Our Captain

No record of the Season 1921/22 would be complete without special reference to the "skipper" of the First Eleven. The name of Mr. George Barnes Senior has figured largely in Sport, and very honourably; the name of Mr. George Barnes, his son, will stand prominently in local Football history for all time. For a young man to captain such a successful side is a credit, but he has the added satisfaction that much of his good work led up to the victories, and the happy feeling existing between himself and his men, and the way he has tried to make all things comfortable, have all contributed to smooth working and success. Here's to George!'

33. Chesham Town Social Club

The Club was first formed before the 1914 War, at the Friends Meeting House, Bellingdon Road, when some of the members meeting there felt that some form of recreation club for young men should be formed – 'to keep them off the streets', I believe, was the reason given at the time. A few simple indoor games were played. Anyone over the age of 14 could join, and numbers soon grew. The Club soon decided that it would like its own premises, and the use of a hut, also in Bellingdon Road, was obtained; this was at the rear of the premises which now house Chesham Coachbuilding Works. Here, a billiard table was acquired, and the game became very popular. I understand that there was always a waiting list of those wishing to play. Dart and shove ha'penny boards were also acquired, and these, together with all sorts of card games, comprised the 'indoor' games that were played throughout the years of the Club's existence. Only men were allowed to join the Club (that wouldn't do today!) and the Club was always 'dry'. Soft drinks, sweets, and later cigarettes were all that was on sale there. A radio or two were later provided.

By about 1930, the Club had outgrown their second premises, which had only been hired, and set about providing their own building. A site in Higham Road was generously offered by Mr. George East, and gratefully accepted. Interest-free loans were sought to obtain the necessary capital. These were soon forthcoming, and the Club's own timber building was quickly erected. Arch Glasgow of Townsend Road, who will, I am sure, be remembered by many, and who was one of the original members from the earliest days, was appointed Steward. Finance was always tight – the members' subscription was six pence per month or five shillings per year. The Club was always open six evenings every week – Monday to Saturday. The Club flourished, and soon had its own Football and Cricket teams.

Our picture shows the Club's Football team at the conclusion of a successful season in the early 1930s – this was taken at Chesham United's ground. The Club itself had the use of a ground at Top Park for both sports (the site is now occupied by Chesham Park

Community College) and also had the use of the Cricket Ground at Vale Farm (the home of Chesham Vale C.C.) where the Thursday team played.

This was in the days when all shops closed on a Thursday afternoon, and the young men employees, who could not play on a Saturday, were glad of a game. In addition to Arch as Steward, two other stalwarts of the 1930s are remembered: Bert Hall, the Secretary, and George Wood, the Treasurer.

The 1939/45 War obviously had a considerable effect on membership, as most of the members served in various branches of the forces, but the young ones – and a few older ones – kept things going, and members on leave could always drop in for a game. In the post-war years, with so many other attractions, membership declined, and the Club finally closed in the 1960s. The site is now occupied by Alpine Caterers.

34. Boating on the Park lake

As we walk through Lowndes Park today, and see the lake, the home of scores of geese, ducks and a few swans, we hardly give a thought to the many pleasurable hours which the lake used to provide, and for the fun which was had there.

From the early 1920s, boating always took place during the summer months. There was little livestock there then, and our Council originally provided just two rowing boats. A landing stage was built at the Blucher Street end, to which the boats were tethered when not in use, and for sixpence for half an hour or one shilling for an hour you could enjoy the pleasure. Fathers would row their children round, with constant calls – 'Sit down, or you will fall into the water!' – and young men would show off their rowing skills to their young ladies. Many a romance I believe blossomed there. Hardly any young man had a car in those days, so local pleasures had to be made.

The boats were in the care of Mr. Reading, the Park Keeper. He lived in a house situate where the conveniences now stand, and always appeared to be on duty. He was certainly feared by the local lads who might have been bent on mischief, and much to his credit, he kept the park in first-class condition and almost completely trouble-free. He would take your money, and time you out, and when your time was up he would call you in. He had a powerful voice, but some lads would pretend not to hear him, and would row off to the farthermost end of the lake. When they did eventually come in, they would almost certainly incur his wrath.

The two boats were soon found to be insufficient, and two more were provided. At night the boats were tethered by the Keeper out on the Island, and he would then row back in a small dinghy, which was picked up and put away in his shed. This stopped the lads from untying the boats, and letting them drift away.

The outbreak of war in 1939 put an end to this simple summer pleasure, and it was never re-instated. Pity!

35. War Time at Pednor

Most of us know Pednor House – or Pednor Castle as it is still known to many of our older residents – up on the hill at Little Pednor, some two and a half miles out of the town, in what is today very rightly designated as an area of outstanding natural beauty. Today it is a very beautiful country residence. Few of us, I am sure, realise what went on there during the early years of the 1939/45 War.

The original house was a farm, but was converted into a private residence in the early years of this century. In 1933 a disastrous fire took place, and, due to the almost total lack of water up there, the Fire Brigade were unable to do very much about it, with the result that the place became uninhabitable. It remained in this state until September, 1940, when, following the great Blitz of London, it was hastily repaired to be used as a maternity hospital by the Royal Free Hospital, whose own premises had been badly damaged.

Between September, 1940, and March, 1941, over

240 babies were delivered at Pednor House, almost all of them to mothers from widely differing parts of London. The mothers were brought down by taxi or ambulance, but the fathers who wished to visit their wives and have a look at their new offspring came down by train, the only means available, there being no petrol allowance for private motorists. There are stories told of fathers arriving at Chesham Station and asking for directions to Pednor House: the address was 'Pednor House, Chesham', and they naturally expected to find it in the town. They were invariably told, 'It's two and a half miles away, along a very narrow road and up a jolly great hill, with no bus service.' So they reluctantly set off on foot, paid their visit, and then had to walk the two and a half miles back to the Station. This did not go down too well with Londoners, to whom a five-mile walk was considered nothing less than a marathon!

Only last year I heard of one mother – now in her 80s – who was delivered there, coming back for the first time to renew acquaintance. On arrival, she asked for direction, fortunately to a local resident, who took her up there by car and showed her around, then took her home to tea before returning her to the Station! Fortunately there are still kind folk around.

Also last year I had a letter from a man, now living in South Wales, who was born at Pednor, and I was able to give him a few details, so, even after fifty five years, interest in Pednor Maternity Hospital is still existent!

36. Early Street Traders

Today we are familiar with the mobile ice cream vendors sounding the chimes from their vans as they travel around the streets in summer, and we have the occasional hawker knocking on our doors. However, the 'old time' street trader of the early years of this century has completely disappeared – the rag and bone man, muffin man, ice cream maker and seller, manure

gatherer and seller and the vendors of home grown produce from horse and cart.

We had several Chesham-based rag and bone men, who called around the streets on a regular basis, giving a few coppers according to how much they collected. Let us remember that, at the time, clothing was all of wool or cotton, both of which were re-cyclable – unlike today's nylon, lycra and other man-made fibres which are not. The Howard family from Berkhamsted called round regularly every Friday – in the early years with a horse and cart, in later years with a lorry. Bones, which were sold by butchers either as a part of 'the joint', or marrow bones, which were sold separately for folk to reclaim scraps of meat, to make soup, or for domestic animals, were also collected for processing in the manufacture of glue – before the days of modern adhesives. Then there was the rag collector, who came round giving goldfish in exchange for rags – children would pester their mother for enough rags to exchange

for a fish – usually a very small one, which was brought triumphantly home in a jam jar. Then there was the muffin man on Saturday afternoons; he also came from Berkhamsted by horse and cart. These would be parked – usually in a pub yard – and a trayful of muffins prepared, covered by a green cloth, the tray then being balanced on the head, and off he went ringing his handbell and crying 'Muffins' in a loud voice. The price was seven for 6d. (2½ pence today). He was much listened for on winter Saturdays, when the muffin, toasted on a fork in front of the fire, made a lovely hot and tasty tea!

Next, we had the ice cream man; the ice cream was for years made locally in a hand-turned machine, packed with ice. Then it was sold from a barrow – usually in the High Street; cornets or wafers at 1d. or 2d., or you could take your own cup and purchase 2d.-worth. By the late 1920s Walls Ice Cream men on their box tricycles appeared, selling a somewhat wider variety, which was factory made – at Acton, London. The 'Wallsie', as he was known to generations of children, usually appeared towards the end of April. Children really felt that summer had come when the cry went up, 'I've seen the Wallsie' – what pleasant memories – we enjoyed the somewhat restricted range just as much as we do the vastly wide range which is available today, when it is difficult sometimes to decide just what to buy!

Then there were the manure gatherers – usually older boys, with a truck made from a Tate and Lyle sugar box on a pair of old pram wheels.

For centuries, all transport was horse-drawn, with the result that large amounts of manure were dropped on to the roads. The boy, with his shovel and brush, would gather this – if possible before it was squashed by passing carts, and it was sold to gardeners as a much-prized fertiliser – before the days of artificials. The usual price was sixpence for a well-filled truck –

a lot of money for a boy – the truck contained upwards of half a hundredweight. This quantity took some time to collect; near to the Town drinking trough in the middle of the Broadway was a prized spot – the horses used to stop there with the inevitable result; timber carts were especially welcome, best of all those drawn by four large horses! With the coming of motor vehicles horse-drawn transport became less and less, and the lucrative side-line for boys gradually faded away.

Finally, there were the sellers of home-grown produce, who came in from the surrounding villages by horse and cart during the growing season with small quantities of home-grown fruit and vegetables including, in the autumn, blackberries from the hedgerows and mushrooms gathered from the fields. Their produce was always fresh, and was much sought after; it provided the producers with a few shillings to supplement their small incomes.

"MANURE GATHERING, AND ICE CREAM STALL, BROADWAY, EARLY 1900S"

37. The Changing Face of Our Industries

I have recently read the brochure which was issued for the Chesham Trades Fair which was held in Darsham Hall (long since departed) in October, 1949.

It lists the manufacturers then existing in the Town, and makes interesting reading, as follows:

Boot Manufacturers
G. Barnes & Sons, Britannia Works
Chesham Boot and Shoe, Higham Road
G. Newton & Sons, Townsend Road
Brewery
Chesham and Brackley Breweries, White Hill
Brush Manufacturers
Beechwood Brushes, Bellingdon Road
Beechy Bucks Products, Severalls Avenue
W. Hawes, Berkhamsted Road
A. O. Lewis, Berkhamsted Road
Modern Brushware, Sunnyside Road,
Robert Russell, Townsend Road
Spa Brushes, Alma Road
Webb, Jarratt, Townsend Road
Cocoa Manufacturers
Van Houten, Asheridge Road
Electro Platers
Chesham Electro Plating, Bois Moor Road
Flag and Regalia Manufacturers
George Tutill, Higham Road
Boiler Manufacturer
Frederick Kay, Nashleigh Hill
Juvenile Tailors
George Williams & Co., Asheridge Road
Laundry
Royal Bucks Laundry, Waterside
Leather Handbags
Shillaker & Co., Alma Road
Manufacturing Chemists
John Furminger & Co., Wey Lane
Kayeff Industrial Products, Wey Lane
Mat and Matting Manufacturers
London Mat & Matting Co., Bois Moor Road
Metal Goods Manufacturers
Amac Refinements, Sunnyside Road

Optical Instrument Makers
Shackman & Sons, Waterside
Pencil Lead Manufacturers
Atlas Pencil Co., Bellingdon Road
Plastics
B. Z. Products, Station Road
Printers
Carlton Press, Broadway
Page & Thomas, Germain Street
Scientific Laboratory Glassware Manufacturers
C. W. Adams, Blucher Street
Soft Toy Manufacturers
H.G. Stone & Co., Amersham Road
Surgical Instrument Makers
H. G. Carsberg & Sons, Asheridge Road
Textile Manufacturers
Kerr Bros., Town Hall
Toy Manufacturers
Amersham Works, Amersham Road
Valve Makers
Hivac, Asheridge Road
Woodenware Manufacturers
J. Bunker & Sons, Hivings Hill
Canada Works, Amersham Road
F. East, Townsend Road
J. East & Sons, Broad Street
Howard Bros., Chilton Road
F. Leach & Sons, Inkerman Terrace
Joseph Reynolds Ltd., Waterside
Sundt, Sundt & Co., Berkhamsted Road
West & Seymour, Bellingdon Road
Woodpecker Ltd., Bellingdon Road
Wm. Wright & Sons, Water Lane
Thomas Wright & Sons, Berkhamsted Road

Of these 47 companies, only three – Newtons, Russells and Tutills – are still in operation 46 years later. Some were companies from London which evacuated here in the war years and subsequently returned there, but many of those which have disappeared had been Chesham names for upwards of a century. I know that there are many older residents today who have memories of working at these factories.

An approximately equal number of companies have set up in the Town, and new companies are still arriving, especially on Asheridge Road, Howard's Estate and at the former Shackman Works in Waterside, but, walking around the Town, I am sorry to see at least a dozen empty factories. Many of these are old Victorian buildings with very restricted access, which is just no use to today's industry, and until our Local Authority change their policy regarding change of use or demolition of these ancient properties I am afraid that they will remain empty, growing ever more derelict and more of an eyesore.

38. The Changing Pattern of Shopping

I have given some thought and research into our Shopping habits of 'Then and Now'.

In Chesham today, apart from those in the 'Main Road' area – Red Lion Street, High Street, Broad Street and Berkhamsted Road – there are only a mere handful of what are termed 'consumer' shops. These are where we shop for everyday necessities. A century ago, and indeed right up until the 1930s, families looked little farther than their own street – or, at least, the next one – for groceries and sweets. A survey reveals that, at that time, and apart from the streets mentioned above, there were at least 50 shops serving their local communities. Half of these were grocers. The rest comprised bakers, butchers, sweet shops, clothiers, boots and shoes, hardware, fish and chips, fruiterers, furnishers, dairies and corn merchants. They were, without exception, privately owned and run, and were very much a meeting place, where local news and gossip·were exchanged – often at great length – a visit would take an hour or so! Very few women were out at work, and, although domestic chores with no modern aids took a lot longer than they do today, there was always time to stand and talk. Everyone knew everyone else's business from gossip.

A good thing, or not? Perhaps it was, as when there was any illness or trouble there was always a neighbour willing to lend a hand, and we did not hear stories of people, mainly the elderly. being found neglected or even dead, as we hear too often today. Another thing was that most people only bought 'for the day'. Money was short – wages in the factories of Chesham were very low at the time – and with no such things as freezers or refrigerators food could not be kept for any length of time, especially in summer.

I suppose that supermarkets were the cause of the demise of the small shop. Our first – Buyright – opened in the early 1950s in the lower part of the High Street, in a comparatively small shop. It almost caused a riot. After much publicity – and quoting prices way below those of the private shops – they opened in a blaze on a Friday morning. There was a queue outside all day long, and by closing time it looked as if a hurricane had hit the place. The shelves were nearly bare. Urgent appeals went out to their suppliers, and the small staff had to work nearly all night as supplies came in, to re-stock for opening on Saturday morning. The shop did not last long – Tesco's soon came to the Market Square – where Iceland stands today – which was less than 100 yards from Buyright, with the result that the pioneer soon fell by the wayside. Then came Waitrose and Sainsburys, and shopping habits in Chesham really changed. A weekly shop, nearly always by car, became the norm as it is today, and the small back-street shops were totally unable to compete. It was said that, buying only in small quantities, they could not possibly compete as the supermarkets bought in huge quantities and could sell at prices which were less than those for which the small shop could buy. The end of an era? Perhaps, but service today is totally impersonal, and shopping is not the pleasant experience it once was.

Another thing is the total disappearance of credit to customers from the shopkeeper; the latter, if he knew that a family were on hard times due to illness or unemployment, would give credit to customers to help them over, and the debt would be paid off week by week when things got better – and no interest charged. The pawnshop has also totally disappeared – just as well! It was a degrading experience for a wife to have to pawn her husband's one and only suit on a Monday morning, to obtain money to buy food for the family, and then having to reclaim it on a Saturday, paying a few hard-earned coppers in interest, when the wages for the week had come in. Jewellery also used to be pawned, and sometimes not reclaimed when things were really bad – what hard times!

39. Chesham Town Silver Prize band

I feel that this book will not be complete without mention of an organisation which was for so many years such a prominent part of the Town's life – the Chesham Town Silver Prize Band.

The band was first formed in the 1880s as the Chesham Brass Band, and, as the picture shows, it was obviously much in demand in those early days.

The picture above shows that the band had, by 1907, become a Silver Band, and is seen marching past 33 High Street, which at the time was the offices of the Urban District Council. The next picture – below – was taken at the end of the Great War in 1918, and shows the strength of the band at that time, and also the full range of their instruments.

The next 20 years were surely the band's heyday; they were very much in demand for shows, fêtes, open air dances, and indeed almost any gathering in the Town and district. They entered competitions in Aylesbury, High Wycombe and Reading, where cups and medals for excellence were won, hence the word 'prize' being added to their title. The band's

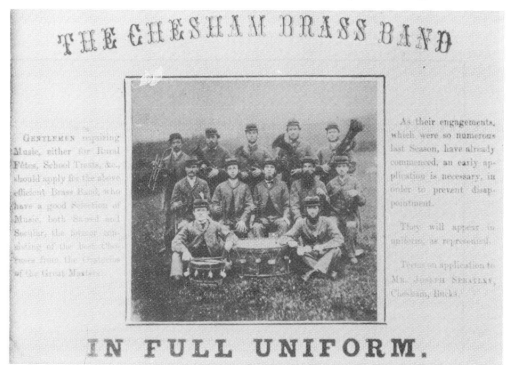

CHESHAM BRASS BAND – 1880s

59

CHESHAM TOWN BAND – 1907.

*CHESHAM TOWN
SILVER BAND, 1918*

THE BAND IN THE 1950s.

KING STREET, 1880s.

headquarters were in a building in Tap Yard, High Street and, throughout the football season, they would march from there to the football ground every Saturday afternoon, playing not only the whole way out and home but also at half time. Many supporters, especially the lads who paid one penny at that time for admission to the ground, followed the band both out and back again; the tune on return was invariably *Colonel Bogey.*

My final picture shows the band in the post-war era, when numbers had begun to decline; this factor unfortunately continued, with virtually no young men coming forward to join, and the band finally faded away in the 1960s.

I close with a few pictures, which I feel may be of interest:

61

VISIT OF GENERAL BOOTH, SALVATION ARMY, TO CHESHAM. EARLY 1900s.

DRILLING FOR WATER AT BECKLEY'S WATERCRESS BEDS.

TOWN HALL AND MARKET SQUARE, EARLY 1900s.

PRAM RACE, BROCKHURST ROAD, 1930s.

ONE OF OUR FORMER DRAPERY SHOPS.

SCHOOLS FESTIVAL, 1854.